The Day
I Didn't Die

by John M. Haffert

LAF
P.O. Box 50
Asbury, NJ, 08802

Nihil Obstat:
Copies of the manuscript were sent to five bishops and to many outstanding Catholic authors and apostles in the U.S., England, and Austrailia. Two copies went to experts in Rome. Specific changes recommended during the ensuing six months were gratefully welcomed and followed.

First Printing: 15,000 copies – 6/98
Printed in the USA by:
The 101 Foundation, Inc.
P.O. Box 151
Asbury, NJ 08802-0151

Phone: (908) 689-8792
Fax: (908) 689-1957

ISBN: 1 890137-12-X

"Write about what you are doing now."

Above are the words the author believes to have heard during a near death experience on July 7, 1996.

His major concern at that moment was the golden jubilee celebration of Our Lady of Fatima as Queen of the World and the decline of the Blue Army. He felt helpless to do much about either. But his heavenly visitors seemed to say that since he was about to write a letter to his sister in Carmel, he should begin with that.

He felt relieved because much of what he would write seemed too personal and too delicate to be published in a book.

Then a year and three months later, in a letter of Oct. 13, 1997, Pope John Paul II called the miracle of Fatima *one of the greatest signs of our times* **because it brings us face to face with the great alternative facing the world,** *"the outcome of which,"* said the Pope, *"depends upon our response."*

To encourage this response in the Blue Army, the author made the decision to publish what he had revealed in the letter to his sister in this book, the entire contents of which can be grasped pretty well from the table of contents, which includes keynote phrases from each chapter.

The figures **7/7/96** throughout the text refer to the July 7, 1996 experience described in the opening chapter.

~~~

COMMENTS

"I just had the blessing of reading *The Day I Didn't Die.* Outstanding work! Your love of Our Mother is contagious and efficacious. Thanks be to God for the perpetuity of your pen and your life."

Dr. Mark I. Miravalle,
S.T.D. Professor of Theology and Mariology,
Franciscan Univ. of Steubenville
President of *Vox Populi Mediatrici*

"I do not doubt the reality of those heavenly visitors on July 7, 1996, in what seemed a near death experience. I am not surprised that they asked you to write about what was happening to you at the moment. Most surprising is that so MUCH was happening!"

Priest advisor to the author

"Over the years I have read almost all your books. With *The Day I Didn't Die,* you have saved the best for last."

James E. Stevens, Retired Executive

"Reading this book I came to believe without doubt that you had a supernatural experience. God wanted this book."

Julia Faco Ceravolo
Founder GEM Television

"Fascinating! I am truly excited about it."

Dr. Rosalie A. Turton, Ed.D.
Founder/Director of the 101 Foundation

"It is good you wrote it! Once begun, one is eager to continue reading."

Rev. Redemptus Valabek, O.Carm.
Editor *Carmel In The World*

"In my opinion this is the best book you have written."

Celeste Behling
LAF Executive Secretary

"Great! I could think of nothing to change."

Dr. Thomas Petrisko
Author

"John Haffert is the greatest Catholic lay apostle/ evangelist of this latter half of the 20th century. In this year of the Holy Spirit, in The *Day I Didn't Die*, he inspires and gives us confidence and direction to become totally consecrated souls, instruments of His Divine Mercy. In the army of His Mother Mary, She will form us as *the saints of the latter days* who, as St. Louis de Montfort said, will form the heel with which She will crush the head of Satan."

Bud MacFarland Sr., M.I.
Nationally celebrated lecturer

"Every apostle in every apostolate, who reads this book, written by one of the greatest apostles of the latter times, will not only be consoled but will be given great hope with a simple formula to bring about Our Lady of Fatima's victory and triumph."

David J. Blum,
Publisher/Editor *Messenger of Divine Mercy*

"I thank God for your near death experience. I could not put it down until I finished reading it."

Anne Bugle,
Pres. Blue Army of Pittsburgh, PA

"I agree with Bishop Jerome Hastrich that you could not die on July 7, 1996. This book is really a treasure."

Rev. Robert Weil
Chaplain of the National Blue Army Shrine
of the Immaculate Heart of Mary

CONTENTS

Above is the giant statue in front of the Blue Army building at Fatima (pictured below). As Queen of the World, while revealing Her Immaculate Heart, She is holding forth the Scapular and Rosary as in the final visions of Fatima. At the top of the building is a statue of St. Joseph as he appeared at the climax of the miracle of Fatima with the Holy Child, blessing the world.

The Blue Army building at Fatima

Chapter One

JULY 7, 1996
THE DAY I DID NOT DIE

My only concern about dying was the
completion of several current projects, one of
major importance. And I was concerned about the
continuity of the Blue Army.

B ishop Jerome Hastrich, former U.S. national
president of the Blue Army, wrote me a letter just
before he died on May 12, 1995. He dictated the letter
to his brother, Father George Hastrich. It was mailed
after the funeral.

The deathbed message gave assurance that the
Bishop, with whom I had worked closely in life
(particularly on the World Apostolate of Fatima,
the Blue Army), would continue to work with me
from Heaven.

On the morning of July 7, 1996, close to my
81st birthday, I awoke with the vivid impression
that I myself was dying. Bishop Hastrich, and other
Heavenly visitors, were at my side.

It might have been a dream; it might have been
pure imagination. I present it as no more than that.
But it seemed to me a supernatural experience
because it was so unusual, so vivid, so lasting.

Bishop Hastrich *was at my side.* In the forefront
among those with him was the former Bishop of
Fatima, the Most Rev. John Venancio.

At first, I thought they had come just to be with me in my last hour. I found myself saying: *"I feel capable and ready to continue my work,* but blessed be the Will of God."

I could not help wondering that God should call me at that moment because I was involved in several unfinished projects, one of which I considered major. But I was at peace, lost in an aura of great light and awareness of Divine Love. In the fullness of that awareness, I prayed: *"Thy Will be done..."*

Write It Down

Immediately after that prayer of resignation, the Bishop said: "God still has work for you to do. *Write about what you are doing now."*

As though he were really there, and as I had spoken to him so freely in the many years we had worked

The author is shown here with Bishop Hastrich just after His Excellency presented to him an award for service to the Blue Army.

together, I protested that I have always considered writing down personal experiences wasteful. Experiences are transitory. The past is past. Is it not more important to focus on what Our Lady is telling us NOW to fructify the hope expressed by the Pope in his millennial encyclical: "The hope of the definitive coming of the Kingdom?"

Only twice in my life had I written at any length about personal experiences. The first was over fifty years before when, to launch the apostolate, I had written *The Brother and I*. Forty years afterwards, at the specific request of my bishop (the Most Rev. George W. Ahr), I reluctantly wrote the history of the Blue Army (1982).

The first book, after I thought it had served its purpose, I refused to have reprinted for many years. And the second, I put off writing for two years until the bishop insisted.

Dear Bishop!

Now, Bishop Hastrich seemed to be saying to me in 1996 what Bishop Ahr had said in 1982: "It is important that you write this. The Blue Army is important to the Church."

In 1982, I had apologized to Bishop Ahr that I would have difficulty remembering. He answered: "You will remember one thing and that will remind you of another."

Incidentally, it may seem that I was imitating Sister Lucia's memoirs in addressing the entire book to the bishop (the title is *Dear Bishop!*) as though it were a personal letter. But that thought never occurred to me. I just felt that to tell my personal experiences would be easier if I were writing just to him even though others would read it.[1]

---

[1] Tens of thousands did. *Dear Bishop!* has been reprinted in English and translated into three other languages.

4

Bishop Hastrich, who in a sense succeeded Bishop Ahr as the Bishop of the Blue Army, *seemed to be giving me a similar mandate.* I understood that he was telling me to *write of what was happening in my life as of that day.*

Again, I exclaimed in protest: "If I wrote of the events happening in my life and *even what has happened in the last three days,* they would fill pages. But would any of it be of lasting interest? There were important things to DO. Was there any importance in writing about *doing* them?

The Most Rev. George W. Ahr, S.T.D., who had been bishop of the diocese of the Blue Army national center from its very beginning in 1950, gave Mr. Haffert a mandate to write the Blue Army history. Since much of it was personal, he decided to write it as a letter to the bishop.

I had two new books[2] about to appear in time for our first national Lay Saints Retreat, which would start just five days later.

For a year I had been working to prepare for the retreat and, at the same time, I was working on the next issue of *VOICE* magazine, which I had been editing since 1993. I had just recently returned from the International Conference in Rome on the proposed dogma of Mary as Co-Redemptrix, Mediatrix, and Advocate (which I was going to feature in the magazine). I was especially involved in an international celebration of the golden jubilee of the coronation of Our Lady of Fatima as Queen of the World, to take place on August 22. And I was concerned about the upcoming (1996) election of national officers of the Blue Army.

What I Was Doing

If I were to write also about the *little* events of the past two or three days (as seemed part of the command to "write about what you are doing now"), they would include a first Friday-Saturday vigil, completion of a novena to St. Maria Goretti (both were yesterday), getting the offices of the Lay Apostolate Foundation ready for the upcoming retreat, an unexpected new printing of my book *Explosion of the Supernatural* (day before yesterday), an article written by the new director of the Blue Army (which came to my attention that same day and caused me great concern), and communications (faxes, letters, telephone calls) related to almost all the events cited above.

---

[2] *Now the Woman Shall Conquer* and an updated edition of *Night of Love*, both published by The 101 Foundation, Asbury, NJ. The first is a sequel to the Sharkey book of similar name, based largely on the messages of Our Lady of All Nations at Amsterdam and Akita. The second is a combined promotion and handbook for all-night vigils.

The cover of this copy of VOICE, of which the author was editor, shows Bishop Varela, a member of the board of sponsoring bishops, presenting a bound copy of past issues of the magazine to the Pope. His Holiness, who had himself introduced the phrase "Alliance of the Two Hearts," told Bishop Varela of his great satisfaction.

Indeed, as I said above, with so many things *to do*, why would I take time out to write about *doing* them?

"The Letter to Your Sister"

As though speaking in mild reproach (as once before Bishop Ahr had told me to remember one thing and then I would remember another), Bishop Hastrich said: *"But you were just about to write to your sister..."*

Indeed, that very day I had intended to write a long personal letter to my sister, Sister Therese of the Queen of Carmel, D.C., in the Boston Carmel. Her feast day (July 16th) was coming next week. I owed her a long letter.

Since this book developed from that letter, a word of explanation:

My vocation, fulfilled especially in the Blue Army, originated with a vision seen by a Carmelite friar in my student days (as told in my book *The Brother and I*), and my sister, believing in this as I did, entered Carmel as my co-apostle. She has been the saint hidden in the cloister, the victim soul who made all the apostolate successes possible.

On my first trip to Europe in 1946, I had a private audience with the Pope, I met the living sister of St. Therese (Mother Agnes), I had a long and unrestricted interview with Sister Lucia, and so on. I found myself saying each morning: "I wonder what *wonderful thing* is going to happen to me today?"

The Victim Soul in My Life

When I returned and went to the Carmel to see my sister, the Mother Prioress said: "We are so glad you are back! The community was wondering each day: 'What *terrible thing* is going to happen to Sister Therese today?'" (Almost daily she had suffered various trials and accidents, such as falling down stairs.)

Day after day, I had been using the very same words with one slight difference: *"wonderful"* vs. *"terrible."*

And now in 1996, only a matter of weeks after the day I did not die, **at the climax of the very events described in this book,** *my sister fell down an iron stair case and was so severely injured that she was expected to die.* The damage to her head was so severe that the brain itself had moved inside her skull. The community was making funeral arrangements.

My brother and I hastened to Boston hoping to be in time to say good-bye. We found our dear sister alive, but unconscious. Were we too late? If she could

Sister Therese of the Queen of Carmel, D.C., sister of the author, who gave up the world in a Carmelite cloister and became the spiritual support of his apostolate.

hear us, we asked her to move her hand. Her hand moved! In amazement, the nurse exclaimed that according to the scan of her brain, what we were seeing *should not be possible.*

Was God permitting her to console us at her departure, even by a miracle of movement?

The Victim Almost Died

My brother and I were stifling tears. The nurse said that our sister's reaction to our voices was a "mystery of faith." The doctors said it was encouraging, but that if she did survive, she would not have the use of her faculties.

Just before the events of which you are about to read, I had a painless near death experience. My victim sister had the pain. And, as in other recorded cases of victim souls, beyond the prognosis of medical science and despite her massive injuries, she not only survived but she recovered her mental capacities completely, and gradually regained use of her limbs. The victim could not die until the work was finished.

Was I right in believing that the Heavenly visitors of 7/7/96 said I would begin to answer their mandate with the long overdue, personal letter I was about to write for her upcoming Feast day?

In any event, the experience had moved me so deeply that I decided to write the letter in greater detail than usual. After that we would see.[3]

As I mentioned, there *were* some major events taking place in my life at that moment. Foremost among them was an international celebration of the Golden Jubilee of Our Lady of Fatima as Queen of the World. It was scheduled to take place only six weeks later.

---

[3] I did not "see" for almost two years. But the conviction that I should write this book persisted. What was written in July of 1996 as a letter to my sister was finally formed into this book in 1998.

Chapter Two

GOLDEN JUBILEE

*That mandate given in the Queenship
encyclical had until now been largely ignored.
Time was running out. If we still ignored it in this
year of the golden jubilee, what might be
the consequences for the world?*

About twelve weeks before 7/7/96, the Honorable Howard Dee[4] had sent me a fax from Manila saying that *he felt impelled to do something important this year (1996) for Our Lady.* His first thought was to have a seminar at Fatima.

At the very time I received his fax, I had been virtually weeping before Our Lady, because I felt almost helpless to do something on an international level to celebrate the GOLDEN JUBILEE *of the coronation of Our Lady of Fatima by Pope Pius XII as QUEEN OF THE WORLD.*

In his encyclical *Ad Caeli Reginam* instituting the Feast of the Queenship of Mary, Pope Pius XII said: "After long and careful consideration, having come to the conclusion that *great benefits will accrue*

---

[4] Former Ambassador from the Philippines to the Holy See, the author of the book *Mankind's Final Destiny,* in which he states that Cardinal Ratzinger told him that the message of Akita is the same as the Third Secret of Fatima.

to the Church... We, by our apostolic power, decree and institute the Feast of the Queenship of Mary... We *command* that on that same day there be renewed the consecration of the human race to the Immaculate Heart of the Blessed Virgin Mary."

As though to emphasize the importance of this command, the Pope added: *"Upon this there is founded a great hope* that there may arise an *era of happiness that will rejoice in the triumph of religion and in Christian peace."*

Just four years before the Pope issued this encyclical, Our Lady was saying in Amsterdam:[5] "Do you know your teaching?" Then She wrote the word ENCYCLICALS in great letters. Then deliberately, She said: "Do you realize how powerful is this force?" (Apparition of Aug. 15, 1950). But the strong mandate, the actual *command* of the encyclical on the Queenship of Mary, had been rarely obeyed.

Now, in these critical years at the end of the century, Pope John Paul II had called upon the Church to be in advent with Mary to the Great Jubilee 2000. *This golden jubilee of Our Lady's Queenship provided a unique opportunity for a final, worldwide response.* The coronation in 1946 marked a turning point in history. *Perhaps 1996 could be another turning point.*

Importance of This Year

In 1946, the year Pope Pius XII had called "the year of decision," His Holiness sent a personal legate to Fatima to crown Our Lady there as Queen of the World. Two years later, I wrote a book about the events of that year titled *Russia Will Be Converted.* One need but run through its pages to verify that this year of the coronation of Our Lady at Fatima as Queen of the World *was a turning point in the history of the world.* And Pope Pius XII understood the important

---

[5] These apparitions, of which we will speak in more detail later, were approved May 31, 1996.

role of Our Lady at that moment in God's merciful plan by crowning Her, at that moment, as Queen of the World.[6]

Other Popes (notably Pius VII and Leo XIII) had made similar coronations. But this time, the Pope made it clear that this was not just the coronation of a statue, but a solemn declaration that *Our Lady of Fatima is Queen of the World.* In his last words to the Cardinal-legate, before the legate's departure from Rome to Fatima, the Pope did not speak of crowning the statue at Fatima. He said: "Remember, Eminence, you are going to crown *The Queen of the World."*

This became more evident after a statue of Our Lady had gone forth from Fatima in 1947 as a "Pilgrim Virgin" to visit various nations. The Pope said: "I crowned Her Queen of the World at Fatima, and the following year She set forth AS THOUGH TO CLAIM HER DOMINION."

It became even more fully evident in 1954 when the Pope crowned the most venerable icon of Our Lady in the western world (the *Salus Populi Romani*) as he instituted the Feast of Our Lady's Queenship. On that solemn occasion, His Holiness said: *"I first crowned Her Queen of the World at Fatima."* And in his encyclical *Ad Caeli Reginam,* issued that day, referring to Our Lady's Queenship, the Pope said: *"In this doctrine and devotion LIES THE WORLD'S GREATEST HOPE."*

All Rome on Its Feet

I was in Rome that day in November, 1954. It seemed that the entire city was on its feet. The procession carrying the *Salus Populi Romani,* which is said to have been painted by St. Luke, filled the streets from side to side all the way from St. Mary Major's to St. Peter's, a distance of more than a mile.

---

[6] The recognition of the Queenship of Mary, as by a crowning of Her images, is an act of consecration. It is saying: "You are our Queen. You have rights over us."

When the Pope crowned that venerable 2,000 year old image and recalled that *FIRST he had crowned Our Lady at Fatima as Queen of the World*, it became stunningly clear that the coronation at Fatima in 1946 was not just a ceremonial gesture. *It was the opening of a new era,* the era of Our Lady of All Nations, the era of the Queen of the World, "to whom," Jacinta said, "God has entrusted the world's peace."[7]

And now, in 1996, we were about to celebrate the golden jubilee of this historic event and no international celebration had even been planned.

Indeed, my heart was weeping when I received that fax from Manila. Twenty five years before, we had celebrated the silver jubilee with coronations of Our Lady in fifty five nations simultaneously around the world. Now, in this golden jubilee, was there to be no international response at all?

My Resources Limited

I was editor of the three year old magazine *Voice of the Sacred Hearts.* But I had no staff. I wrote most of the articles, and even used personal resources to cover expenses. I was privileged to have this VOICE to promote devotion to the Sacred Hearts, but it was still too small to implement an important international project. And our apostolate of the Alliance of the Two Hearts was still in its infancy.

In addition to the magazine, the only other support I had was from the 101 Foundation, which had agreed to lead a pilgrimage to Fatima for the jubilee. We were planning a ceremony honoring Our Lady's Queenship at the castle near Fatima. That was all.

What was our little magazine, the pilgrimage, and the castle ceremony, compared to the resources we had at the time of the silver jubilee, including: *SOUL* magazine with many thousands of readers, the Blue Army in over a hundred countries, and the Bishop of

---

[7] *Her Own Words to the Nuclear Age,* p. 172.

Howard Dee, while ambassador to the Holy See from the Philippines, is shown here with Pope John Paul II.

Fatima personally accompanying us on preparatory visits to all six continents of the world?

Howard Dee Had the Resources

But, while I no longer had those resources, Howard Dee had a large staff and financial resources. And, having been the ambassador of his country to the Holy See, he could open important doors. His message (that he felt compelled to do something important for Our Lady in this year) made my heart soar with hope. It was beyond coincidence.

I replied at once that we could try to *organize coronations of Our Lady around the world* as renewal of consecration to the Immaculate Heart of Mary on the feast of Her Queenship, thus fulfilling the mandate of *Ad Caeli Reginam*.[8]

---

[8] The encyclical issued by Pope Pius XII in 1954, in which the Pope instituted the feast of the Queenship of Mary.

The feast (August 22) was now less than eight months away. It did not seem that there was time enough for anything worldwide. I suggested that we ask for *participation of the Holy Father and,* because of the shortness of time, *aim for a simultaneous international telecast.*

Necessary at This Moment in History

I faxed off the message to Manila. Pius XII had solemnly mandated renewal of consecration to the Immaculate Heart of Mary on the feast of Her Queenship in the same encyclical, in which he had said: *"In this doctrine and devotion lies the world's greatest hope."* That mandate given in the Queenship encyclical had until now been largely ignored. Time was running out. If we still ignored it in this year of the golden jubilee, what might be the consequences for the world?

Within a few days, Howard replied that Cardinal Sin agreed to head up an International Committee. His Eminence would ask the Holy Father to participate and we would then invite all the Marian Shrines around the world to join in this Queenship program with the Pope. Ambassador Dee asked me to form the committee.

Was it going to be this easy?

Chapter Three

JUBILEE CELEBRATION

*The Perpetual Memorial to the
Queen of the World at the Fatima Castle
became the focal point for the worldwide
celebration of the Golden Jubilee.*

In the beginning, I spoke of "Heavenly Visitors" on 7/7/96. Only Bishop Hastrich spoke, but close beside him was Bishop John Venancio (second bishop of Fatima and first elected international president of the Blue Army), with whom I had worked for the celebration of the Queen of the World's *silver* jubilee (1972). We had arranged for simultaneous coronations of Our Lady in 55 countries...

For that celebration, we had prepared *three years* in advance, with personal visits by the bishop to all six continents. But now, for the more important *golden* jubilee, we had *less than eight months* to prepare!

And, to hinder and delay us, there would certainly be the powerful agents of spiritual warfare.

Satan Fears the Queen of the World

The silver jubilee celebration in 1972 had ultimately been a very great success, and certainly an event of special grace for the world. (Indeed, when we get to Heaven we may be surprised to discover

The Most Rev. John Venancio, Bishop of Fatima, being addressed by the author, who worked intimately with the bishop for the international Fatima apostolate. The bishop became the Blue Army's first elected international president.

how important it was.) And naturally, since this was a spiritual victory, we had incredible opposition.

Satan is Satan. Affirmation of Mary's Queenship *is conditional to the triumph of Her Heart.* ***That is synonymous with Satan's defeat.***

But, Our Lady was crowned *simultaneously* on that silver jubilee day of May 13, 1972, in fifty-five countries around the world! There were coronations in Moscow and Prague, in Hungary and Germany, in literally all the major capitals of the world, usually by the foremost Cardinals or Presidents of Episcopal Conferences. In the United States, the national Shrine of the Immaculate Conception was overflowing when the Cardinal Archbishop of Washington did the crowning there. And, despite all opposition, the Holy Father participated by radio and television. (Just the highlights of this worldwide event fill all of Chapter 25 of *Dear Bishop!*)

But now, for the golden jubilee, those who had given most help for the silver jubilee (especially Bishop Venancio and Father Balic, former head of the Pontifical Marian Academy) were dead. Someone else was in charge of the Blue Army. I had a small magazine,[9] as mentioned above, but without even a single assistant. So it seemed a direct intervention of God when Howard Dee offered his services "out of the blue."

Faxes were going back and forth between Manila and our home almost day after day. I was getting up at night to write, hoping not to disturb my wife. But it was getting difficult. Several times the fax machine would start in the middle of the night. And just when it seemed that everything was conspiring to discourage us, a fax came from Father Melada, who had succeeded Father Balic as President of the Pontifical Marian Academy in Rome. In effect it said: "Go for it!"

To understand the importance of this, one needs to understand the importance of the Pontifical Marian Academy. It is considered the "right hand of the Pope" in things Marian. Its quadrennial international congresses are often attended in person by the Holy Father and are always the platform of a special message from the Pope.

Now Could Anything Go Wrong?

Shortly after the committee was organized with participation of half a dozen different Marian apostolates, Howard had to go to Europe for a conference. When he returned to Manila he found

---

[9] Perhaps, in God's Providence, one of the reasons we had the magazine (*Voice of the Sacred Hearts*) was for this purpose. Shortly after the jubilee celebration of 1996, the Philippine group had developed personnel to take over the magazine and I was no longer editor.

For the celebration of the silver jubilee of the crowning of Our Lady of Fatima as Queen of the World, the bishop of Fatima, shown above at left, traveled to fifty-three countries around the world to present statues of Our Lady of Fatima in anticipation of the jubilee. Here the author holds the statue being presented to His Holiness, Patriarch Athenagoras, head of the Orthodox Catholics of the world, in Istanbul. "You have brought me great joy," said His Holiness. "You have brought my Mother."

that, in his absence, his committee had decided to join in a major celebration with the Pilgrim Virgin in Manila on the following May 13, 1996,[10] rather than become involved with a worldwide event in August.

Newspapers said that *two million* participated in that one great event in Manila with three Cardinals and many bishops participating in the crowning of Our Lady. But we wanted similar recognition of Our Lady all around the globe rather than just in Manila. And now all our hopes for an *international* celebration seemed shattered.

We sent overnight letters and faxes to all the Episcopal conferences of the entire world. To our amazement, we learned that a similar movement had started in France and was spreading to other nations. It was called "The Pilgrim Virgins."[11]

A few months before our initiative, the Holy Father had blessed 250 statues and icons from various countries, which were to be carried in each nation from parish to parish for vigils of prayer. Before the end of 1996, seventy countries were involved.

This apostolate of traveling images of Our Lady was not directly linked to the Golden Jubilee, but it was *as though Our Lady Herself was again reaching out as Queen to the nations of the world.* As said above, seventy countries responded.

Simultaneously, we hoped to focus attention on the significance of 1996 as the golden jubilee. Symbolic coronations were arranged on all five

---

[10] Since the Pilgrim Virgin was scheduled to visit the Philippines, at that time the combined Marian Apostolates decided to concentrate on that May 13 celebration. Estimates of the crowd reached two million gathered on that one day.

[11] This international effort is sponsored by *Notre Dame de France*, 48 Ave. de Paris - F - 91410 Dourdan (Fax: 33-1-64-596522). Materials available in English. Climax of the campaign, Sept. 8, 2000.

Waving banners of WELCOME MAMA MARY tens of thousands of Filipinos welcome the International Pilgrim Virgin

APR-MAY'96 *of the* **SACRED HEARTS**

VOICE

This cover of VOICE shows the welcome given to the International Pilgrim Virgin in the Philippines. On May 13, 1996, two million are reported to have participated in the ceremonies in Manila, perhaps the greatest single demonstration in honor of the Queen of the World in history.

continents. Everything was centered around the August 22 event, which had already been prepared at the Fatima Castle of Ourem.[12]

Event Planned at Fatima Castle

As mentioned earlier, even before Howard Dee had been inspired to do something special for Our Lady for the golden jubilee, we had planned a celebration of the Queenship on the Feast, August 22, at the Castle of Ourem. This is the castle of Fatima, closely linked to the entire story of Fatima and in a special way to Our Lady's Queenship, as we shall explain in a little more detail later.

In 1646, the King of Portugal had placed his crown at the foot of a statue of the Immaculate Conception. He proclaimed Her Queen and vowed that never again would a Portuguese monarch wear the crown now given to Her. He commanded that stone plaques be placed into the walls at the gates of all the castles in the realm as a perpetual memorial of this proclamation.

Tens of thousands of Fatima pilgrims have passed through the gate of Ourem Castle and looked at that proclamation of 1646 engraved in the centuries-worn stone. Just opposite, visible from that spot, one sees the tower of the Basilica of Fatima where, in 1946, on the actual third centennial of the giving of the crown of the Kings and Queens of Portugal to Mary, Pius XII crowned Her *Queen of the World.*

---

[12] Fatima is in the County of Ourem. The Castle, on a mountain opposite Fatima and visible from the place of the apparitions, was the center of government in this area for more than 2,000 years. The castle town was severely damaged in an earthquake in 1755 and the government moved to a site below. It is there that the children of Fatima were imprisoned and threatened with death on August 15, 1917. Fatima was dependent upon Ourem for courts, law enforcement, fire protection, etc., and the Castle was its proud landmark.

One of the old towers of the Castle of Ourem, the seat of religious and civil authority in the region of Fatima for more than a thousand years. The Basilica of Fatima can be seen from the castle walls, about 3 miles away.

Now, celebrating the golden jubilee of that coronation in 1996, we had arranged for a monument to be built adjacent to the castle towers from where both that stone, engraved with the king's 1646 proclamation, and the Basilica of Fatima are visible.

Success

That monument at the castle became a focal point for the worldwide celebration of the golden jubilee.

On the previous Nov. 1 (1995), all Saints day and anniversary of the death of Blessed Nuno (who had been the Count of this castle of Ourem), the base of the monument was blessed by the Prior of Ourem in the presence of the Duke of Braganza, direct descendant of the King who, 350 years before, had given his crown to Our Lady. (The Duke would be king today if the monarchy were restored.) He was also a direct descendant of Blessed Nuno, "Our

Unveiling of the monument to the Queen of the World at the Fatima castle on the Feast of Our Lady's Queenship in 1996. The ceremony was the focal point of a worldwide commemoration of the golden jubilee of the papal coronation of Our Lady of Fatima as Queen of the World.

Lady's Knight," who is called the Precursor of Fatima and who was the third count of this Fatima castle.[13]

On 7/7/96, I was looking forward (just six weeks to the day) to when *a large golden crown*, offered by two hands in the shape of doves, *would be mounted upon that tower on August 22* in perpetual commemoration of this golden jubilee of Our Lady, Queen of the World.

I leap ahead for a moment to tell of a marvelous sign Our Queen gave at that moment.

᾿A crowd, including over a hundred U.S. pilgrims, saw a wonder in the sky at the very moment His Royal Highness, the Duke of Braganza, the direct descendant of the King of Portugal who had given the crown to Mary 350 years before, unveiled the monument.

As I begin to tell this amazing story, I wonder at the fact that, were it not for my "Heavenly visitors" a few weeks before, this would perhaps have remained unknown.

Joyous moment just after the crowning, in Red Square, of the International Pilgrim Virgin by members of the 1992 world youth congress, in Moscow. It was the climax of almost a half century journey through the world to Russia, launched by a world youth congress at Fatima in 1947.

---

[13] The writing of the biography of Blessed Nuno, *The Peacemaker*, pictured on page 163, is what brought me into contact with the first Bishop of Fatima. It was the first biography of this saintly hero in English. Blessed Nuno is also known as "the George Washington of Portugal."

Chapter Four

SIGN OF JOY

*At the moment of the unveiling of the
monument to the Queen of the World at the
Castle, a large crowd (including over 100 U.S.
pilgrims) saw what seemed to be a miracle.*

At the moment of the unveiling a shout had gone up: "Look at the sun!"

It was not the first time I ever saw a disc in front of the sun, or that the sun seemed to pulsate. But now, not only were both phenomena occurring, but there were most amazing and brilliant colors. I had never known or seen any similar phenomenon in all my 81 years.

I took it to be a sign of Heaven's joy.

At that moment, as we were honoring Our Lady at the Castle of Fatima, the coronations we had arranged were taking place on all six continents. And on this very day of Our Lady's Queenship, through the special efforts of Howard Dee, *the International Marian Congress* at Czestochowa in Poland *was passing a resolution* **to promote consecration to the Sacred Hearts in all the dioceses of the world.**

Sun Pulsated

Over a hundred pilgrims were there from the United States. I asked for written testimonies. A witness from Hartford, Connecticut, testified: "I saw the sun pulsating while a disc, like a Host, appeared in front, and beams of light shot forth from its sides. I staggered in amazement. Prior to this Fatima experience, I was not a practicing Catholic. This has deeply changed my devotion to my faith, Church, and to the Blessed Virgin. Since then I have attended Mass almost daily, and I now practice adoration daily, and say the Rosary two to four times each day."

One can imagine how great was the supernatural impact of this event which caused a non practicing Catholic not only to return to the Sacraments but to frequent attendance at Mass, to DAILY visits to the Blessed Sacrament, and to praying more than two Rosaries a day.

Never Before

Armantine Keller, a very well educated and sensible woman from Memphis, Tennessee, whom I have known personally for many of her seventy-plus years, wrote: "Never before in my life have I experienced anything so beautiful."

The inscription on the monument being unveiled at that moment reads as follows: "On the Gate of this Castle is the declaration of 1646 when the King of Portugal gave to Our Lady Portugal's Crown. From here you see Fatima, where 300 years later (1946), the Pope crowned Her QUEEN OF THE WORLD. This monument, dedicated on the Golden Jubilee of that coronation by the Pope, is a lasting memorial of gratitude to our Queen for Her promise that 'An era of peace will be granted to *mankind.*'"

Saw Our Lady

Gena Ehrhardt from Gallaudet University in Washington, D.C., after describing the disc in front of the sun and the brilliant colors, writes that at the moment of the unveiling of the monument she saw: "a silhouette of Our Queen entering the sky from behind the sun... Her arms were extended downward.

Instantly, I wanted to kneel. I was in amazement and awe. *I felt that Our Lady came to receive Her crown."*

Several others said that they also saw Our Lady. I wondered why all of us had not seen Her. Was it because we were so dazzled, perhaps even struggling with unbelief before what we saw?

Charles and Janet Papst were there with their son, David. Mrs. Papst said she was looking at the tower of the Basilica of Fatima, marveling at the unusual aspect of the sky. "Then suddenly," she said, just before the unveiling of the monument, "wide bands of rays shone through the clouds over the countryside of Fatima. It appeared as if *Mary was standing to the right side of the Basilica with Her arms extended downward* (as on the Miraculous Medal)... Just as the Duke stepped over to unveil the monument, *the sky opened up*, like an eye opening in the clouds, and at that moment *the sun looked as if it was covered completely by a Eucharistic Host...* It was as if the

A shout went up: "Look at the sun!" Notice the pilgrims looking up into the sky, as colors and rays come from and on the pulsating sun.

Blessed Mother wanted this special moment to be shared with the world!"

Never Before

Many of the witnesses, who said they had seen similar phenomena on other occasions, said that nothing equaled this. For example, Dr. Rosalie Turton, President of the 101 Foundation, who could be considered a specialist in such matters, writes:

"Sky and sun shimmered and sparkled as if covered with silver dust. The sun itself was blue. I have seen the so called "miracle of the sun" many times before, particularly in Medjugorje, but this was the first time I ever saw a blue sun," (also seen by Mr. Lee Havey, future seminarian, and others).

Dr. Turton remarks on the importance of the fact that not only was this witnessed by so many but that *it happened at the very moment of the unveiling of the monument to Our Lady as Queen of the World.*

"I Witnessed A Miracle"

Ashley Puglia, of Springfield, Illinois, says: "When I tell people *I witnessed a miracle at Fatima,* there are widely different reactions. Some react with disbelief: 'You all must have been hypnotized.' Some nod their heads as if they want to believe but know better.

"Nevertheless, on August 22, 1996, feast of the Queenship of Mary, in Ourem, Portugal, I saw the sun dance before my eyes."

After describing what she and so many others saw, Ashley says: "I think it was Mary exulting over Her worldwide celebration. The experience filled all who witnessed it with a great sense of joy, thankfulness, and love. I feel quite blessed to have been a witness to this miracle."

She added, writing several weeks later from her home in Illinois: "My impression of the solemnity and uniqueness of what I saw has increased with the passage of time."

Sign of Hope

I have spoken at length in my last book, *Now the Woman Shall Conquer,* of the great promise of Our Lady of Fatima: "Finally My Immaculate Heart will *triumph*...an era of peace will be granted to *mankind.*" (Emphasis added.) It may have been *this promise of world peace* which prompted Pope Pius XII to crown Our Lady at Fatima as Queen of the World.

St. Catherine Labouré, to whom Our Lady revealed the Miraculous Medal (in the very manner several witnesses said they saw Her during the unveiling of the monument at the Fatima Castle), exclaimed prophetically at the dawn of the Marian Age:

"Oh how wonderful it will be to hear Our Lady hailed as Queen of the World! It will be a time of joy, peace and prosperity."

"It Will be a Time of Joy"

The prophecy of St. Catherine Labouré (that *when Our Lady is hailed as Queen of the World,* we will see Her triumph) is a special sign of hope. Pope John Paul II said that, as we approach the millennium, "it seems the *words of Our Lady of Fatima* are nearing their fulfillment," and that we make that approach *"in the hope of the definitive coming of the kingdom."*

This is one reason why I said at the very beginning that affirming the Queenship of Mary at this time was perhaps more than a mere option but something we *had* to do. And, not because of the saint's prophecy, but because of an ensemble of events (eminently including Fatima and Akita), and the long ignored encyclical *Ad Caeli Reginam.*

We affirm the Queenship of Mary every time we crown one of Her images. We acknowledge that, as our real Queen, *to whom "God has entrusted the peace of the world"* (Jacinta), She has *rights* over us. She has a right to direct us. She has a right to our service.

God has entrusted the peace of the world to our Heavenly Queen, but as Pope John Paul II stressed in a special letter to Fatima of Oct. 13, 1997: *"Her promise is conditional to our response."*

At the end of this book, we will review the essentials of the response. The Fatima pledge is especially for those in spiritual lethargy. But Our Lady is calling us all to greater holiness. Even mystics need to respond more. The more we respond, the more the grace.

In *The Dogma and the Triumph* (Queenship Publishing Co., 1988, 153 pgs.), Dr. Mark Miravalle writes: "In an authentically Marian sense, we have reached the fullness of time. We have reached that which has been called the climax of the age of Mary, an apex, a summit, a high point which has been preceded by many holy events and great saints and teachers."

It is the time of the lay saints as described by St. Grignion de Monfort. The Blue Army was formed to give us those saints. The sooner and bigger the response, the sooner and greater the victory.

Permanent Memorial

As witnesses testified, many felt that the wonder witnessed at the moment of the unveiling of the Queenship monument at the Fatima Castle was a sign from Our Lady that She was pleased with the coronations and ceremonies which took place that day on all the continents of the world and, perhaps above all, with the consecrations to the Sacred Hearts around the world which would follow in the wake of the resolution of the International Marian Congress.

As a result of this worldwide celebration, in addition to the monument unveiled that day, a permanent museum to the Queen of the World was established within the castle walls. It is supported by a small percentage of the offerings from the travels

Garden in front of the museum in honor of Our Lady, Queen of the World, at Ourem Castle. Shortly after this picture was taken, a monument was erected in the garden dedicating it to the Most Rev. John Venancio, the second bishop of Fatima, as "the Bishop of the Queen of the World."

of the International Pilgrim Virgin, "the messenger of Her royalty" (Pope Pius XII).

The museum, of which we will speak briefly again in Chapter 21, is to be found around the corner from the Cathedral, fronted by a public garden dedicated to *"the Bishop of the Queen of the World,"* the Most Rev. John Venancio, one of my Heavenly Visitors of 7/7/96.

Our Lady's Crowns

This perpetual memorial to the Queen of the World will contain symbols of Queenship with which Our Lady appeared through the ages, such as the triple crown She wore at Pontmain, the crown of roses surmounted by shafts of light worn at La Salette, the golden crown at Beauraing, etc...

At Rue du Bac and Fatima, the symbols of Her Queenship were the globe of the world on which She crushed the serpent, and then, the second apparition with a smaller globe, of which She said to St. Catherine: "This globe represents the world and each particular person."

Of special interest is the crown Our Lady wore in Her apparition over Red Square in 1992 when the International Pilgrim Virgin was crowned there in Moscow. The crown She wore *was like the crown used at that moment to crown Her statue in the square below.*

Interestingly enough, that crown had been borrowed from a statue of the Infant of Prague...the *Infant King,* crowned and holding the scepter and orb.

I remember every detail of this vividly because, completely by surprise, I was the one who crowned the statue that morning in Red Square.[14]

I could not help but wonder if Our Lady arranged this because, as a founder of the Blue Army fifty years before, I could represent *all those more than twenty five million who had made the pledge to fulfill Our Lady's requests for the conversion of Russia.*

Moreover, it was as though Our Lady had literally accepted the crown from Her Son-King, as She appeared transformed in brilliant golden light in triumph over Red Square.

When we crown an image of Our Lady on earth, is it not accepted in Heaven?

---

[14] On this same day, there were TWO coronations in Red Square. The first was in the presence of our some 1,000 pilgrims during the day. For this, a small statue was used and it was at this coronation that Our Lady appeared. The second coronation took place at midnight in front of the tomb of Lenin at the changing of the guard, in which members of the World Youth Congress participated in crowing the International Pilgrim Virgin...at which moment another wonder occurred. See book *Finally Russia,* published by The 101 Foundation, Asbury, NJ.

When we crown an image of Our Lady on earth, does
this not resonate in Heaven? Above is a painting of the
coronation of the Virgin which the author discovered in
the Chiesa Nova in Rome where St. Philip Neri is buried.

Chapter Five

LOOK INTO HER EYES!

*The reception in the Philippines, on
May 13, 1996, may have been the single greatest
demonstration in honor of Our Lady ever to have
taken place in history.*

The crowning jewel of the permanent memorial to
the Queen of the World at the Fatima Castle is
the miraculous statue pictured on the back cover of
this book. It was blessed at Fatima on Oct. 13, 1947,
to be an "International Pilgrim Virgin." Whenever the
statue is not traveling for a given length of time,
it will be enshrined at our Queen's permanent
memorial in the Castle of Fatima.

As mentioned in a previous chapter, all the
apostolates in the Philippines decided to join together
for the crowning of this statue in Manila on May 13,
just a few weeks before 7/7/96.

We had made the decision to send the statue
to Asia not many months before, following a dis-
agreement between the custodian of the statue
(Mr. Carl Malburg) and the new direction of the
Blue Army.

We were deeply disturbed by this conflict, but we
were consoled by a wonder which took place at
that moment (which will be described shortly), and
by remembering the words spoken to me by the first

Bishop of Fatima when the Pilgrim Virgin set forth on Oct. 13, 1947: *"Our Lady will make Her own way."*

One of several Providential results of this trial was that the Pilgrim Virgin received a new crown *like the one with which Our Lady appeared triumphantly over Red Square in 1992,* most solemnly placed on the statue at the end of the 1997 Peace Flight in the presence of almost a thousand pilgrims, who had been in Moscow on Oct. 13, the actual day of the golden jubilee of the Pilgrim Virgin.

The International Pilgrim Virgin. Various photograhs show changes of expression. More than thirty times tears flowed from the eyes.

Problem So Grave

Another Providential result was that reception in the Philippines on May 13, 1996, which may have been the single greatest demonstration in honor of Our Lady *ever* to have taken place in history.

But, despite these blessings, on the day I didn't die (7/7/96), the problem just mentioned seemed *so grave* that I sadly wondered whether the travels of the miraculous statue *might be coming to an end.*

Then, on the Feast of Our Lady Lourdes (after I decided to write this book), I thought I heard Our Lady say: "My light will shine through the darkness to many."

That same day, I got a call to arrange for the statue to be on the Eternal World Television Network with Mother Angelica live.

Mother Angelica, who had been crippled for forty years, had been cured during recitation of the Rosary just two weeks earlier. Those now watching *Mother Angelica Live* were in the millions. On this program the miraculous statue would "visit" thousands of homes. Her light would shine to many.

Looking into the eyes of the Pilgrim Virgin, one remembers that more than thirty times they shed tears before many witnesses. Her glance seems mixed with sadness and concern. She is an anxious mother who comes—to use the very words of the recent letter of Pope John Paul II: *"to save man from himself..."* And the Pope added: *"Beneath Her maternal mantle, which extends from Fatima over the whole world,* humanity senses anew its longing for the Father's house and for His Bread (cf. Lk. 15:17)."

Perhaps the reader already knows the story of the Pilgrim Virgin, but since my mission in this book is to tell what I was doing on 7/7/96, perhaps it is God's Will that I summarize it here. And I will tell of something so unbelievable that were it not for what happened on 7/7/96, it would not be told.

To Travel from Nation to Nation

The reader will recall that when Pope Pius XII instituted the feast of the Queenship of Mary at St. Peter's in Rome, His Holiness said: *"I first crowned Her Queen of the World at Fatima."*

The following year, 1947, an international youth congress at Fatima resolved that a statue of Our Lady of Fatima, "Queen of the World," should travel from nation to nation across the world to Russia.

The Bishop of Fatima consulted with Sister Lucia to whom Our Lady of Fatima had appeared. She suggested sending a new statue which had been recently made under her direction by a sculptor named Thedim.

Miracles Were Seen

Miracles of conversions and cures began to occur along the path of the statue as it began to travel across Europe. It was front page news.

At my request, the Bishop then asked Thedim to make another statue to be used *specifically as a PILGRIM VIRGIN.* And in October, just six months after the first statue had set forth, the Bishop blessed the "Pilgrim Virgin" before hundreds of thousands at Fatima. It was traveling in America from diocese to diocese when the Pope, amazed at what was happening, mentioning America, said: "I crowned Her **Queen of the World** at Fatima *and the following year, through the Pilgrim Virgin, She set forth as though to claim Her dominion and the favors She performs along the way are such that we can hardly believe what we are seeing with our eyes."*

The Rev. Dr. Joaquim Alonso, member of the Pontifical Marian Academy and official documentarian of Fatima, said: *"Never in the history of the Church have charisms descended in such abundance on the people of God* as through the **Pilgrim Virgin:** the miracles of healing, conversions of hearts, movements of masses of people gathering to honor the Virgin *without precedent in the religious history of the Church.* It caused the Pope to speak of the marvels which the Pilgrim Virgin has wrought throughout the entire world."

Most astounding have been the millions who gathered for the visits of the statue in countries where, as the Holy Father himself remarked, only a small percentage were Catholics.

I was privileged, with the Bishop of Fatima himself, to accompany this Pilgrim Virgin statue around the entire world three times, and once around the continent of Africa. Unbelievable though it be, I have seen the statue smile and I have also wiped a tear from its cheek.

It is about the smile that I would not have written were it not for this book, because certainly readers would think it was imagination. But, I hope what I am about to say will be as much a source of joy to you as it was to me.

Loreto Statue Smiled for Pope John XXIII

Let me first speak of one of the only other times I have heard of a miraculous smile. When a wooden statue changes expression without being touched, it cannot be explained naturally.

It was when Pope John XXIII went to Loreto in fulfillment of a promise to make a pilgrimage there for the success of the Vatican Council. As he knelt before the solid wooden statue in the Holy House, it smiled. Photographs recorded it. The Capuchin Fathers who serve at Loreto thought it might have been an accident of lighting. After the Pope's visit, they photographed the statue over and over in various positions and with constant changes of light. Only after exhaustive tests were they convinced that a miracle had taken place.

But what a joyful miracle! What a consolation to this wonderful old Pope who dared to convoke a Council of all the bishops of the world despite opposition on all sides. At the very moment he had

Quand tout va mal...

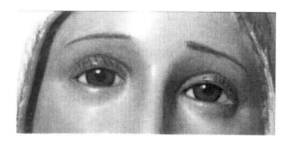

...il y a encore quelqu'un qui peut vous aider

Millions of copies of this picture of the eyes of the International Pilgrim Virgin have been circulated throughout the world with a message in many languages (the above in French): "When all goes badly...there is still someone who can help you. Look into Her eyes!"

Then the folder opens and the full picture of Our Lady's face can be seen.

announced the Council, he said he would go to Loreto to ask Our Lady's intercession. When he died during the Council, he asked that his ring be placed on that statue through which Our Lady gave him the consolation of Her smile.

The Pilgrim Virgin's Smile

It was during the grave circumstance that caused our decision to send the Pilgrim Virgin to Asia that a group of six of us were amazed, and infinitely consoled, to see the International Pilgrim Virgin smile.

I had seen the statue many times in the previous fifty years. I thought on more than one occasion that it seemed to change expression—sometimes very sad, sometimes just grave. Aside from the times tears flowed from the eyes, I might have thought the changes of expression were imagined.

But on this occasion, the change was so dramatic that it was absolutely stunning. Not only did the corners of the mouth raise but her whole aspect was one of *smiling*. Carl Malburg, the official custodian of the statue, who had been traveling with it day after day for several years, joined in our amazement.

What a consolation it was to see Our Lady's image, so often grave, so often seeming on the verge of tears and at times shedding them, now smiling!

And it was at a moment of great concern... although not a concern which could have matched that of the saintly John XXIII when he went to Loreto to ask Our Lady for the success of the second Vatican Council.

We did not look on Her smile so much as approval of what we were doing, but as a remembrance of Her promise despite all opposition: "Finally My Immaculate Heart will triumph." And of the words of the old bishop: "Our Lady will make Her own way."

Look Into Her Eyes!

Millions of pictures of the statue in full color have been distributed literally *all over the world* on a leaflet with the title: *Look into Her eyes!*[15] The leaflet, which originated in Brazil, explains that these are the eyes of a statue, but not just of ANY statue. These are eyes of the International Pilgrim Virgin, which have shed tears as She traveled the world "to claim Her dominion."

The Pope said that it seems to be truly Our Lady Herself who has gone forth to remind Her children of the conditions which must be met if we are to have the triumph She has promised.

In the special letter issued for the 80th anniversary of the miracle of Fatima, the Pope said[16] that in the

Finally ... Russia! by John M. Haffert

*Haffert's book **Finally...Russia!**, part of the cover of which is shown here, has a hundred color photographs together with the amazing story of the arrival of the Pilgrim Virgin in Russia after traveling the world **towards that specific destination** for almost fifty years. It tells of an apparition of Our Lady over Red Square on this occasion.*

great sign of this miracle, **we are presented with an alternative: war *or* peace.** He says one of the main reasons Fatima is one of the greatest signs of these times is *"because its message announces many of the later events and conditions them on the response to its appeals."*

We will not have the promise without the response. *And Our Lady seems to be traveling the world to evoke our response.*

Indeed, visits of the Pilgrim Virgin carry a special responsibility. As the Holy Father has said, the triumph depends on OUR response. And if we have had Our Lady's visit, do we not have a special obligation to respond? Can we look into Her eyes and still ignore Her message?

After some 25 million persons around the world responded by making the basic pledge (promoted especially along the path of the Pilgrim Virgin), we had the dissolution of the Soviet Union.

Apparition Reported Over Red Square

When the Pilgrim Virgin was in Moscow in 1992, accompanied by almost 1,000 pilgrims,[17] Our Lady is reported to have appeared over Red Square as She appeared at Fatima, but this time wearing a crown.[18]

---

[15] It is promoted in the U.S. by *America Needs Fatima* with headquarters in York, PA. In more than 20 other countries, it is promoted by TFP which was founded in Brazil. It's members live the *Totus Tuus* consecration of St. Grignion. Because of TFP's open campaign against Communism and Liberation Theology in Brazil, they were accused there by some bishops of disobedience. In a letter of May 24, 1997, Cardinal Stikler wrote from Rome that after investigating all allegations *"with extreme care and diligence,"* he gave TFP full support. The highly placed Roman Cardinal said of TFP's detractors: "I am bewildered and sad that such false-witness takes place in circles that should be united and concentrated on the defence of our great common cause of the Church."

[16] Osservatore Romano, Oct. 29, 1997

From Her Hands and Her Heart great rays of light streamed down to the square and then flared up and out in every direction.[19] It was "a brightness you could not describe" and it seemed as though the whole world was being bathed in this light.

Our Lady continues to tour the world "like an anxious mother," as the late Bishop Luna, President of the World Apostolate of Fatima, put it. She is anxious, as Pope John Paul II said in his Oct. 1997 letter, "to save man from himself."

The very day the Holy Father issued that letter (October 13, 1997), the Pilgrim Virgin was in Moscow. It was the anniversary of the day She had left Fatima just 50 years before.

Becomes a Special Occasion

At each visit, in dioceses and parishes, the statue is the occasion for a renewal of consecration to Her Immaculate Heart, as the statue is crowned in recognition of Her Queenship. This follows the spirit and the mandate of the encyclical of Pope Pius XII on the Queenship of Mary. It is so important that, even though we have quoted it before, we quote it again. The encyclical says:

"In this doctrine and devotion of Our Lady's Queenship *lies the world's greatest hope." It requires that*

---

[17] This pilgrimage, using two jumbo jets, was organized by The 101 Foundation and the International Alliance of the Two Hearts.

[18] In February of 1998, I asked the person who saw this vision about the crown. The description she gave was identical to the one she had given me in Moscow almost six years before. The crown was gold, similar to the crown which was placed on the statue during the golden jubilee trip to Russia in 1997. And around Our Lady's head like a halo were twelve brilliant stars. Our Lady's robe and mantle were white, edged with golden light, as at Fatima.

[19] For further details, see book *Finally Russia!* published by The 101 Foundation, Asbury, NJ.

each year on the feast of Our Lady's Queenship "there be renewed consecration to Her Immaculate Heart."

The same encyclical refers to the statue of Our Lady of Fatima as **"the messenger of Her royalty."** These visits of the Pilgrim Virgin, like the Feast of Her Queenship, provide special occasions for carrying out the mandate of the Pope and the resolution of the International Marian Congress of August 23, 1996: To promote throughout the world the **consecration of every heart and every family to the Sacred Hearts of Jesus and Mary.**[20]

---

[20] The only condition for scheduling the statue is permission of the Bishop for individual pastors to invite Our Lady to visit. The statue itself is accompanied by a full time custodian. It is recommended that the sponsoring persons or apostolate follow up with the PVE2000 program within the diocese. The International Pilgrim Virgin Committee (P.O. Box 50, Asbury, NJ) provides kits and information.

Chapter Six

SIGNS OF TRIUMPH

In that Golden Jubilee Year,
fiftieth anniversary of the coronation of
Our Lady of Fatima as QUEEN OF THE WORLD,
wonderful things happened.

While I have been writing about the major events in which I was involved on 7/7/96, let me skip ahead to the end of that year to look back at a few of the signs of hope it left with us.

Wonderful things happened, some of which are bound to have lasting effects:

(1) *the Feast of the Immaculate Heart was elevated to an obligatory memorial;*[21]

---

[21] This, in the context of the message of Fatima and the promised triumph, was of great importance. Our Lord had told Sr. Lucia that the reason He insisted on the collegial consecration of Russia to the Immaculate Heart of Mary was so that "all the world will know that this favor (the conversion of Russia which was promised to take place when the consecration was made) was obtained through the Immaculate Heart of My Mother, so that afterwards *devotion to Her Immaculate Heart will be placed alongside devotion to My Own Sacred Heart.*" The Church placed the Feast of the Immaculate Heart immediately following the Feast of the Sacred Heart, but until now it had been merely a memorial. (Incidentally, the change in Russia took place only ten months after the collegial consecration. See my book *Her Own Words.*)

(2) *the public cult of Our Lady of All Nations was approved;*

(3) *The permanent memorial to the Queen of the World was dedicated at the Fatima Castle;*

(4) *In a message to the 12th International Mariological Congress, the Pope said* it was fitting now to proclaim Mary Mediatrix;

(5) There was *a resolution of the International Marian Congress* (largely through the efforts of Howard Dee) *for a three year project* to consecrate individuals, and especially families, to the Sacred Hearts throughout the world.

Importance of This Resolution

This resolution by the official international Marian Congress was signed by the Cardinal legate of the Pope and by the President of the Pontifical Marian Academy, together with other officials of the Congress. Copies were sent to *all the episcopal conferences throughout the world.* Years from now, the implementation of this resolution may prove to have been an important factor in the triumph of the Sacred Hearts and for the success of the Pope's plan leading the Church into the millennium "in the hope of the definitive coming of the Kingdom."

The resolution of that Congress, if implemented, *could really bring to the world the triumph promised at Fatima in the new millennium.*

To help implement the Congress resolution, the World Apostolate of Fatima initiated a marvelous program developed by Sister Mary Francis, A.M.I.[22] This program combines the home Pilgrim Virgin devotion with the millennial encyclical *Tertio Millennio Adveniente.* Details can be obtained from the Blue Army, Washington, NJ, 07882.

---

[22] *Ancillae Mariae Immaculatae,* The Handmaids of Mary Immaculate, a community founded in 1953 primarily to assist and to promote the Fatima devotion through the Blue Army.

The same program is being promoted throughout the world along the path of the International Pilgrim Virgin—the statue which Pope Pius XII called "the messenger of Her royalty." It is also promoted by the International Alliance of the Holy Family, especially in third world countries.

Pope's Message

In his special message to the top theologians from all over the world assembled at that International Mariological and Marian Congress, the Holy Father said: "On **the threshold of the third millennium we wish to draw near in** *a special way* **to the Mother of God...**"

The Pope then surprised many by saying: **"It is right that the Church should attribute to Her the title of Advocate, Helper, and also Mediatrix."**

These are titles which over fifty years ago the Lady of All Nations had asked the Church to recognize with the promise that, *when they are defined, Her triumph will begin.* And we recall again that St. Catherine Labouré, to whom Our Lady appeared as Queen in 1830, prophesied: "O, How wonderful it will be to hear Our Lady hailed QUEEN OF THE WORLD! IT WILL BE A TIME OF TRIUMPH..."

Is This to be Hoped NOW?

Is this the hope seen by Pope John Paul II when he asked us to be in advent with Mary in these critical years in *the hope of the definitive coming of the Kingdom*?

Let us stop to realize that in the last half of the 20th century, our Blessed Lady has led her children through a very difficult passage. We not only survived the second world war (which Our Lady of Fatima had foretold), but we have been continually protected while constant threat of atomic destruction hung over us like a sword of Damocles.

The Most Rev. Andreu Koudrusiewicz, Archbishop of Moscow, embraces the author at a thanksgiving Mass at the Blue Army Shrine in Washington, NJ.

How Explain Russia?

After all the dangers of these years, came the almost bloodless dissolution of the Soviet Union, an event which the Pope said seemed hardly able to be explained, except in the context of the message and prophecy of Our Lady of Fatima, the Queen who promised the conversion of Russia and the triumph of Her Immaculate Heart.

And what will we say of the attempted assassination of the Pope *on the actual anniversary day of the first apparition of Our Lady of Fatima,* which he not only survived but which he commemorated by having **the actual bullet placed in the crown** of our Lady at Fatima, *the very crown with which Pope Pius XII just fifty years ago proclaimed Her Queen of the World.*

The Pope has spoken often of being saved by Our Lady from the assassin's bullet. The doctors said that the trajectory of the bullet changed in an unexplained manner after it struck the Pope, avoiding vital organs.

On Feast of Her Queenship!

And it was actually **on the Feast of Our Lady as Queen of the World,** August 22, 1990, *that the Russian people brought down the Soviet Marxist regime.* The following Christmas day, the hammer and sickle came down from over the Kremlin, never to be lifted again. But was the danger now over?

In his recent book *The Last Crusade*, Dr. Thomas Petrisko said: "*It cannot be overemphasized* that it was on October 13 (the anniversary of the miracle performed at Fatima "so that all may believe"), that Our Lady appeared as *Our Lady of All Nations in Akita,* Japan, in 1973, and said that fire will come upon the earth in a chastisement *worse than the deluge* if people do not mend their lives, but that *so far She (the Lady of All Nations) has been able to hold it back."*

She has shown Her power. **She has shown with the change in Russia, immediately following the requested collegial consecration, that She can change nations and alter the course of history. She can keep Her almost unbelievable promise: "An era of peace for** *mankind."*

But She asks, She requires, our cooperation.

The Bishop of Akita said: "She reminds us that weapons capable of wiping out entire nations are not only still viable but spread in more and more areas." **Now a special response is needed** by those who believe. This becomes a responsibility for all of us. In the mind of the founders it is the reason for existence, and therefore a special responsibility, of the Blue Army.

Let us keep in mind that OUR LADY OF ALL NATIONS, speaking at Akita through a miracle of tears, said She has "so far" been able to hold back the chastisement.

And now, back to our story:

The Trivia

To make sure that all would be ready at the Fatima castle for the Queenship Feast (August 22) of this year of the day I did not die, I had gone to Fatima on May 10.

On the feast of Our Lady of Fatima (May 13), the papal legate was Cardinal Pironio, head of the Council for the Laity with which I had corresponded for years about the Blue Army and the Lay Apostolate Foundation. And this was *the actual day on which, fifty years before, Pope Pius XII through his legate (Cardinal Masella) crowned Our Lady Queen of the World.* To be at Fatima that day was indeed a special grace. Meanwhile, Dr. Mark Miravalle had invited me to participate in the *Vox Populi* leaders conference in Rome, which opened May 31, 1996. Since everything was going well at the Castle, I accepted to attend the conference.

What a grace this turned out to be! It was primarily about this that I was going to write to my Carmelite sister on the day I didn't die, although I would have considered many of these details too trivial to be shared beyond the pages of a personal letter.

Chapter Seven

HER CRUSHING HEEL

For reasons difficult to fathom, beyond the fact of spiritual warfare, there has been almost incredible opposition to this dogma and to events like the crowning of images of Our Lady around the world.

I n this same year of the golden jubilee of Our Lady's Queenship (1996), on the very day of the opening of the Rome conference on the proposed dogma of Mary as Co-Redemptrix, Mediatrix, and Advocate, **the apparitions of *Our Lady of All Nations* in Amsterdam were approved.** The Queen of the World seemed to be taking things into Her own hands! This is the subject of the book *Now The Woman Shall Conquer*, which was about to be released within the week of the day I did not die.

One of the three Cardinals who spoke at the Conference on the dogma was Cardinal Gagnon (whom I greatly admire, as one can gather from almost an entire chapter citing him in my book *You Too! Go Into the Vineyard!*).

His Eminence said: "We were told that it was not necessary to proclaim this a dogma because it is something all Catholics already believe. But it is also necessary to *proclaim* what we believe."

Seen here at the Vox Populi Congress in Rome on June 2, 1996, left to right, are the author (in shirtsleeves), Cardinal Dos Santos, Cardinal Gagnon, and Dr. Mark Miravalle.

Why the Opposition?

While most bishops of the world may feel the same, Cardinal Gagnon was one of the five hundred bishops (including forty-one other Cardinals) who dared to disregard the almost overwhelming wave of opposition which seems largely to be based on the opinion that some might think we were making Our Lady's participation in redemption and mediation EQUAL to that of Jesus. But a co-pilot is not the pilot. Jesus is our Sole Redeemer and Sole Mediator. Mary redeems and mediates WITH Him.

But since Our Lady said at Amsterdam that the moment the dogma is proclaimed Her triumph will begin, obviously *there will be all the opposition Satan and his legions can muster.*

Only in this light of spiritual warfare (here I am expressing a purely personal opinion) can we understand how a commission of theologians appointed by the Pontifical Marian Academy could unanimously oppose the dogma. It is almost like a defiance of the Pope by his Marian "right hand."[23] In his message to the 1996 International Marian Congress, sponsored by the Academy, the Pope had indicated that it was time for this dogma to be proclaimed, and one would have thought that any commission of the Academy would have complied.

I spoke of this to Father Melada, O.F.M., President of the Academy, who had encouraged us to go ahead with the international plans for the golden jubilee of Our Lady's Queenship. As mentioned before, I had worked closely (and successfully) with his predecessor[24] for participation of the Holy Father in the worldwide coronation event of 1972. And it was with the help of Fr. Melada that we had set up the Committee on the Alliance of the Two Hearts about nine years before.

He spoke frankly: "They (those opposing the dogma) do not want even to *hear* about this dogma. All they want is affirmation that Mary is the Mother of God. That contains *everything*."

But on May 31, 1996, Our Lady Herself provided a great sign of encouragement when, *on the very day that the conference opened, the Most Rev. H. Bomers, Bishop of Haarlem (which includes Amsterdam)* **approved the public cult of Our Lady of All Nations**...the Lady

---

[23] However, it is to be noted that this was not a decision of the Academy but only of a small commission of theologians appointed by the Academy. If the entire Academy of 80 theologians had been polled it is almost certain they would have decided otherwise. But, in this atmosphere of spiritual warfare, the decision of this commission was even mistaken to have been the decision of theologians convoked by the Vatican itself. Knowing the true facts underlines the truth that Satan will go to any length to prevent Our Lady's triumph.

[24] Father Balic, O.F.M., who was primarily responsible for the encyclical *Ad Caeli Reginam.*

whose image shed tears and came to life at Akita...the Lady who had said in Amsterdam that *this dogma would usher in the era of Her triumph.*

Good People on Both Sides

Off and on through these pages, I will be speaking of the new dogma and of the need for it now. But also through these pages, we will encounter this spiritual warfare, so difficult to define and yet so blatantly real.

It is not that those who oppose recognizing the Queenship of Mary, or oppose definition of Her attributes of Co-Redemptrix and Mediatrix, are not good and often devout people. In the crises and divisions that arise, there are usually good and sincere people on both sides. Father Basile Moreau, the founder of the Holy Cross Order, had been the spiritual father and caring superior of the very men who came to think of him as their enemy rather than their father, when the Order was brought by Satan to the brink of dissolution.

How do we explain it? Why does God permit it?

The answer of course is as simple as the phrase: No pain, no gain. But from the hill of advanced years, I can see from experience another reason.

Satan sows discord. He creates incidents, he insinuates thoughts, he cultivates misunderstandings. He does it most to the persons whom God chooses for special work, like Fr. Moreau of whom we will speak in a coming chapter. Satan tries to destroy a work by destroying the person chosen by God to perform it.

But what is the result?

Ultimately the very divisions Satan creates usually lead to proliferation of good works.

We find this in dozens of examples, similar to that of Fr. Moreau, in the development of the Holy Cross community and as we do in the struggle over the last Marian dogma.[25] Good invariably comes out of it.

If there were no opposition to the dogma, would there be millions of petitions streaming into the Vatican? Would we have these wonderful conferences which *explain* the proposed dogma and *bring it into our devotional life?*

Satan is crushed by the heel of Our Lady the more he strikes against it.

I will be coming back to this subject because, I must confess, it has preoccupied me a great deal in these last years. But I would like to take a moment now to share what proved to be (although I had not thought of it at the moment) the personal golden jubilee of my own vocation.

*Left to right: Dr. Turton, Father Bing (executive director of the Alliance of the Two Hearts), and John Haffert. Fr. Bing often speaks of **spiritual warfare**, which seems to be reaching a climax in our time.*

[25] The reason for choosing Fr. Moreau's experience as an example of spiritual warfare will be explained later in Chapter 14.

Chapter Eight

A PERSONAL JUBILEE YEAR

When I told my wife (who likes to hear such things), she said: "You must write and tell your sister." And that is why it is here, although it is something I would not normally repeat.

Just fifty years before 7/7/96, *almost to the very day*, I had met Sister Lucia[26] and started the "March of Pledges." I had also been to Rome where, in a private audience, I received the consent and blessing of Pope Pius XII.

Now just before 7/7/96, the day of my Heavenly visitors, I had been back to Rome for the conference on the last Marian dogma.

Fr. Redemptus Valabek, O.Carm., Carmelite Postulator General, invited me to stay at the international "mother house" of the Carmelite Order. And, as told in *The Brother and I*, this was the very place I had thought I would be assigned when I was planning to become a Carmelite priest over fifty years before. It seemed that fifty years were swept away.

In the simple room of that old Roman monastery, I felt "at home." I had lived the most important

---

[26] Sister Lucia, eldest of the three children of Fatima, was at the time with the Dorothean Sisters near Porto. The following year she entered the Carmel in Coimbra.

Father Redemptus Valabek, O.Carm., presenting guests to the Holy Father on the occasion of the beatification of Blessed Isidore Bakanja in April of 1995.

formative years of my youth in a similar room with a bed, desk, chair, wardrobe, bookcase, and a wash basin with hot and cold water. The other facilities were down the hall. Normally it would be the "home" of a Carmelite priest assigned to study or work in Rome.

Heightening the illusion that I was back in Carmel was the fact that, for the success of the Queenship jubilee, for a month I had been abstaining from all television and reading only spiritual books.

Downstairs was the Blessed Sacrament chapel with an enormous stained glass window over the altar showing Our Lady giving the Scapular to St. Simon Stock. And I was given access to the big library where my angel led me to a certain book, as I will describe in a moment.

It was odd. It was as though what I had thought would happen fifty years before was happening now.

Meeting an Old Classmate

As I passed down the corridor on the day of my arrival, through an open door I saw an elderly priest working at a computer (the way monks of old would have been printing parchment). He saw me and rose. Suddenly I recognized him. "Joachim!"

He had already recognized me although we had not seen each other for more than fifty years. We fell into each other's arms.

The two friars to whom I had been "closest" fifty years before, *during eight formative years* in Carmel, were Marcellus and Joachim.

I exclaimed to two other priests who were there: "Joachim was my hero. He was not only a gifted poet and writer, but he"...and I went on to tell them about an incident in football when Joachim almost bit through his tongue tackling a runner from behind.

Fr. Joachim has become the historian of the Order. The two of us went out for a pizza to talk over old times. I told him how one day Marcellus and I were walking together and Marcellus asked:

"To what day are you looking forward most in your life?"

I answered, "The day of my profession" (because that was the day I would totally separate from the world with vows of poverty, chastity, and obedience to belong wholly to God).

Marcellus stopped short and exclaimed: "And NOT the day of your ORDINATION?"

I remarked to Joachim that it seemed to indicate even then that God had marked a different path for me than that of becoming a priest.

"But I would have given the same answer," Joachim said. And in his turn, he remarked that ever since ordination, he had been here in Rome in the Generalate, and the few times he had administered sacraments of baptism and marriage were for members of his family. He had stayed close to Marcellus through the years. Marcellus was a holy man and had become novice master. But God had taken him at an early age.

The Lay Apostolate

Yes, in those ten days in the international mother house of the Carmelite Order, just a few weeks before 7/7/96, I was at "home." How grateful I was to Fr. Redemptus...whom I had not known except by correspondence because he was considerably younger. He was now responsible for the Lay Carmelite apostolate, the third Order, and editor of *Carmel In The World*. In my late-in-life effort to do something for the lay apostolate, he had much to share with me. He said to me early in the week:

"Once a week I speak to the *Donum Dei* Community and I would like to have you tell them of your personal experience."

Donum Dei, which has over 400 members, eighty of whom are in Rome, are trained laity in the world. Fr. Redemptus feels that it is a concept of tremendous importance to the future vitality of the Church. He introduced me as: "The man who has done more to make the Scapular Devotion known than all the Carmelites in the world today."

When I told my wife (who likes to hear such things), she said: "You must write and tell your sister." And that is why it is here, although it is something I would not normally repeat.

But perhaps it is proper that it be told because it shows there are certain areas in which a lay apostle can be effective. But at the same time, let it be said that if I was effective in the lay state, I am sure it was only because I was prepared by eight years (plus two[27]) of Carmelite formation. That is one reason

---

[27] I left the seminary just before solemn vows, but then taught in another Carmelite seminary for the next two years, during which my spiritual formation continued under the direction of my lifelong spiritual director, who was novice master there.

why our Lay Apostolate Foundation so much stresses apostolic formation.

Certainly a major reason for the phenomenal success of *Donum Dei* (and there are other lay apostolates like it) is FORMATION.

Frank Sheed stressed in many of his writings, and especially in *The Church and I,* that lay apostles must be "formed" as are persons in religious life. *Donum Dei* members are sent to three houses of formation for a total of nine years before receiving a "mission." (Examples of their missions, and the obvious need for formation, are cited in my book *You, Too!*)

We will speak of this again when I come to write of the Lay Saints retreat which took place only four days after 7/7/96. But now continuing with that letter to my sister, however little relevance it may seem to have, let me continue to tell about those days in Rome.

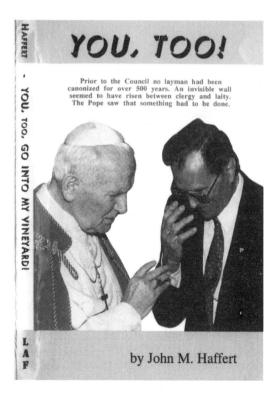

HAFFERT

• YOU, TOO, GO INTO MY VINEYARD!

L
A
F

YOU, TOO!

Prior to the Council no layman had been canonized for over 500 years. An invisible wall seemed to have risen between clergy and laity. The Pope saw that something had to be done.

by John M. Haffert

Chapter Nine

TIME OUT FOR ROME

I have always had a nostalgia for Rome,
which I felt could never be satisfied. It is so old
and yet seems always new. Although I was there
for the Vox Populi Congress and to promote
the golden jubilee coronations around the world,
Rome came alive with memories.

E ven outside the *Vox Populi* Congress the days in
Rome were precious. With a one week bus pass I
went to almost all the places dearest to me: The four
Basilicas—once to St. Paul's, twice to St. Mary Major,
several times to St. Peter's, which is literally just
down the street from the Carmelites (twice seeing the
Pope), and St. John's, where now, as in St. Peter's and
St. Mary Major, there is a chapel of Adoration.

I even got out to Tre Fontane, to the place of the
martyrdom of St. Paul, and to the Shrine of Our Lady
of the Revelation—site of a modern apparition, which
I had visited frequently during those five years of the
Second Vatican Council when I had an apartment in
that part of Rome.

All over the Eternal City, thanks to Pope John Paul
II, I found chapels of Adoration in addition to the
traditional ones, the most magnificent being of course
the one with the effigy and arm of St. Peter Julian
Eymard only a few steps from Santa Maria in Via,

The author in front of the Carmelite Church on the avenue leading down to St. Peter's. He felt "at home" in the motherhouse of the Carmelite Order, the Order in which he had studied fifty years before.

with the miraculous well upon which floated a terra cotta image of Our Lady.

Experience at the "Lourdes of Rome"

Three times, although briefly, I got to S. Andrea delle Fratte, where Our Lady appeared to Ratisbonne and which Benedict XV called "the Lourdes of Rome." St. Maximilian Kolbe chose to say his first Mass at that altar of the apparition, and once I had an extraordinary personal experience there twenty four years earlier concerning Padre Pio and the Blue Army.

I had left the world peace flight in 1972 to go there to say a prayer that the flight would hasten the triumph of the Immaculate Heart of Mary. I had very little time because I had left the group of more than a hundred with local guides, so I intended to say only a brief prayer.

But I was struck by the attitude of the priest who was saying Mass at the altar of the apparition. It was near the end and I decided to wait and ask him to celebrate a Mass for the triumph of the Immaculate Heart.

To make a long story short, the priest turned out to be the celebrated Capuchin, Fr. Andrea D'Ascanio.[28] When I asked him to say the Mass he told me that he was on his way from Naples to Milan and he had stopped off in Rome just to say this Mass at the altar of the apparition, and his intention was *for the triumph of the Immaculate Heart of Mary.*

Suddenly he said to me: "Are you a member of the Blue Army?"

I was amazed. I was wearing a trenchcoat with no outward insignia, and he had never met me. He reached in his sack and produced Blue Army pledges in Italian. Then he asked: "Do you know who is the founder of the Blue Army?"

Before I could overcome my amazement, he said that the *spiritual* founder of the Blue Army was Padre Pio.

Padre Pio recognized the Fatima pledge as a special gift from Our Lady to enable souls to escape from spiritual lethargy. He said he would accept *as his spiritual children* all those who lived up to their Blue Army pledge.

This today is a special treasure. The Blue Army pledge is now the only sure way of knowing one can become a spiritual child of Padre Pio.

Millions have signed the pledge for the triumph of the Immaculate Heart of Mary. When Padre Pio is canonized and better known, many may also sign it to become his spiritual children, of whom he said: *"I will wait at the gates of Heaven until all my spiritual children have entered."*

---

[28] Founder of the White Army and of an international apostolate of God the Father: *Edizioni Pater,* Box Mail 135, 67100 L'Aquila, Italy.

Venerable Padre Pio, stigmatic priest of the Capuchin Order, agreed to accept as his "spiritual children" all who would live up to the Blue Army pledge.

Indeed, one of the very great advantages of joining the Blue Army is the spiritual sharing with all other members. Among them are souls like Mother Teresa (who, with her whole community, was one of the early members), and Blessed Isidore Bakanja, martyred because of his devotion to the Scapular and the Rosary.

Thousands who lived the pledge are now in Heaven. I felt that I had experienced the presence of many of them on the day I didn't die.

Our Lady of Victories With Us

This meeting with Father D'Ascanio was too unusual to have been mere coincidence. The Queen of the World plane had just landed in Rome and, trusting that I would still have enough time to get to the hotel before the group, I rushed in a taxi all the way into the city *to this particular church*...just one of MANY Marian "shrines" in the eternal city. And *at this same time* Father D'Ascanio had interrupted his trip from Naples to Milan to *visit this same church*, and *for the same intention:* the triumph of the Immaculate Heart of Mary.

I persuaded Father D'Ascanio to go with me to the hotel where I introduced him to the Bishop of Fatima and asked if he would work for the Blue Army in Italy. The bishop was so impressed that he and I went later to speak of this to the Capuchin Prior General. Father D'Asanio founded the complementary "White Army," with the same pledge for children. It spread all over the world.

In spiritual warfare, Our Lady of Victories *draws us together.* She said at Akita that, "so far," She has been able to hold back the chastisement by offering the Passion of Her Son to the Father, with the help of *"beloved souls who console Him and form a cohort of victim souls."*

Power of Victim Souls

Only in Heaven will we know the debt we owe to the generous few who accept the call of victimhood. "Lightning rod of God" was the name given by Jesus to Alexandrina. This could also be said of Bertha Petit, Theresa Neumann, and Luisa Picaretta (all three, like Alexandrina, lived many years solely on the Eucharist). And there are the almost forgotten ones like Little Rose Ferron, Rhoda Wise, and so many others *of our own time*, often unknown.

It so happens that all these voluntary victims just mentioned were lay persons. There must be many

Above is the bed on which Alexandrina lay as a victim, consuming nothing but the Eucharist during the last thirteen years of her life. Over her bed is seen Our Lady of the Scapular of Mount Carmel. Jesus called her "the lightning rod of God."

more in religious life, like my dear sister in Carmel, who offer *everything.*

We may not all respond with the gift of *everything,* but we are all called to live the morning offering, to sanctify the actions of *today.* When we take our first wobbly steps on this path to sainthood with the morning offering, Our Lady holds us by Her two hands of the Rosary and the Scapular.

This was the "pledge" Father D'Ascanio had in his sack when we met with the same intention: The triumph of Her Immaculate Heart.

Her Glorious Title

I wrote a separate book about this. I might have titled it *First Step to Sainthood.* But instead I called it: *Her Glorious Title.*[29]

Although not based on Garabandal, for which a final miracle of confirmation was awaited, *Her Glorious Title* explains that Our Lady came at Fatima and elsewhere today as *Our Lady of Mt. Carmel* to invite us to take that *first step in the ascent of Carmel*: The Fatima pledge.

As I said, Rome has so many memories. I do not tire of recalling those which are connected to Padre Pio and to the power of the Fatima pledge to put all the world on the way to the triumph promised at Fatima.

Guardian Angel Guide

I got to so many favorite places by a maze of different bus routes that I think my guardian angel must have helped me on and off the right busses.

Even if one were to spend years in Rome, there seems always something new to discover. This time, when I went to Santa Maria Ai Monti to visit the tomb of St. Benedict Joseph Labré, patron of the Lay Saints Retreat, for the first time I also visited the house in which he died and in which one of his major miracles took place.

Thinking often of Blessed Anne Marie Taigi, the other major patron of LAF, I went to churches which had been dear to her: Ara Coeli and S. Andrew of the Valley, both places where Our Lady appeared to her;

---

29 AUTHOR'S NOTE: I accept no royalties or payment of any kind for my books, so there is no self-serving reason for mentioning them, as I do from time to time, in the hope that the reader will be led to them.

St. Marcellus where a confessor told her of her lay vocation and where she was married; St. Maria in Via Lata (where St. Paul was in house arrest for two years), the church she most frequented and where now, as in so many other important churches of Rome thanks to Pope John Paul II, there was adoration.

I went to Mass at the Chiesa Nova, where St. Philip Neri is buried, and knelt right by his tomb over which the Mass was said. The church was resplendent in flowers and ornate draperies. The day before, the Church of Rome had celebrated *the third centenary of his death*. There was a big story that same day in *Osservatore Romano*. Here, I "discovered" the beautiful painting of the coronation of Our Lady in Heaven which is to be seen at the end of Chapter six.

Yes, even though I once had an apartment in Rome for five years and have been there at least fifty times, I have never gone back without discovering something new.

This time, in addition to the house of St. Benedict Joseph mentioned above, I visited the somewhat remote so-called French church, whose dome is one of the most prominent in the skyline. On a wall, enclosed in glass, was the cross which St Philip Neri used to carry in the streets of Rome. As I gazed at it, I realized that my really "new" experience of this visit was a deeper meeting with St. Philip, founder of the Oratory. As I had knelt at his tomb in this third centenary of his death, I wondered if we did not all need to know him better for the needs of the Church today—like that of the Marian Movement of Priests.

I called St. Paul's abbey to meet a truly close friend of fifty years, Fr. Anastasius Pernitzky.[30] I was

---

[30] I met him at the Russicum in Rome in 1946 and we had been close friends for ensuing fifty years. He was a great devotee of Padre Pio, a brilliant man fluent in several languages, and a gifted artist. He was a monk at the Basilica of St. Paul when he died later this same year.

dismayed to learn he had become ill and was in a hospital outside Rome. Three times I called the hospital. Three times I was told I could not speak to him. Was he dying?

I went to the abbey. I could get no detailed information. I was planning to get to the hospital (by now very much worried) when I got a telephone call from Father Anastasius! He sounded fine! He said he had been unable to receive my phone calls because he was in an area without private telephones. He had a stroke and was in for rehabilitation but expected to be out in good time and back to work at the Abbey. I was so relieved!

The author with his lifelong friend, Father Anastasius Pernitzky, at the Monastery adjacent to St. Paul's Basilica in Rome. Father Anastasius had written on the back of the photograph: "Remembering the father of the Blue Army on the occasion of the golden jubilee of our friendship." It was dated August 20th, 1996, shortly before his death.

Since I was leaving the next day, we made do with a telephone visit. It was the last time we spoke in this world. Later that year, at the same time of my sister's almost fatal fall, he died. In my bedroom is a large and very beautiful picture he painted for me of the Immaculate Heart of Mary, over which Padre Pio prayed before blessing it. I frequently call on him especially when I prepare to receive Holy Communion. I feel that he helped me with this book.

Old, Yet Always New

Of course there are the "other" sights of Rome. I found the Trevi Fountain bright and clean, but FULL of tourists. I stopped in at #10 Via d'Umilita, where 25 years ago I arranged the "coup" that gave us the participation of Paul VI in the worldwide celebration of the Queenship of Mary. And at the top of the Spanish steps, I treated myself to lunch on the Hassler roof, which offers one of the best views of Rome. I had stayed in that hotel 50 years ago almost to the day. (I was shocked at the new prices!)

On another day I lunched in the Piazza Navona, opposite the church of St. Agnes where St. Therese was "given" a ceiling tile for her sister Pauline (in Carmel, Mother Agnes), whom I had met in Lisieux in 1946—another personal golden jubilee remembrance. Pauline was Therese's "little mother."

From Piazza del Popolo I climbed up to the Pincio and walked along the hill with its "aerial" view of the Eternal City, past the Medici Palace to the Spanish stairs. And on my way back "home" to the Carmelite motherhouse, I went to Piazza Essedra to see once again the last great work of Michelangelo, the vast and magnificent church (formerly the baths of Diocletian) in honor of Our Lady of the Angels, the Queen of the World.

I could go on for pages—that is what Rome is like. And I have always, always had a nostalgia for Rome which I felt could never be satisfied. It is so old and yet seems always new.

Another "new" thing for me this time were the baths of Trajan, which for many years had been closed but have now been turned into a wonderful museum. I wandered for over an hour during which two thousand years faded into *now*.

Speaking of that recalls that on more than one Christmas in Rome, I made it a point to go on Christmas eve to the tomb of Augustus, an experience which has always helped my meditation on the third joyful mystery of the Rosary.

The two thousand year old tomb of this most powerful man in the world, who sent out the edict which fulfilled God's Prophecy that Jesus was to be born in Bethlehem, is behind St. Charles Borromeo's church (which contains St. Charles' incorrupt heart). At the tomb of Augustus, I was at *the reality of Our Lord's birth.*

Aerial view of St. Peter's where the author attended the vigil of Corpus Christi and the next day celebrated the feast at Fatima.

74

This time without planning it, while waiting for a bus, I found myself with time to pray the joyful mysteries while gazing at the Emperor's tomb. It was one of those unexpected graces one finds in the eternal city with its relics of the past at every turn.

My last day in Rome presented another unplanned gift. I assisted at beautiful Solemn Vespers in St. Peter's for the vigil of Corpus Christi, a very special feast in my life as mentioned in my book *The World's Greatest Secret* (and further explained in Chapter 18 of this present book). The very next day, I was at Fatima, the Shrine of *Our Lady of the Eucharist*,[31] for the feast itself.

But I had not come to Rome to satisfy a personal spiritual hunger. I had come for the *Vox Populi* Congress and to make important contacts in Rome for the celebration of the golden jubilee. We wanted coronations in every nation.

---

[31] May 13, the Feast of Our Lady of Fatima, is also the Feast of Our Lady of the Eucharist. The apparitions and message of Fatima are primarily Eucharistic.

Chapter Ten

SIGNS AND COUNTERSIGNS

Satanic signs proliferate in the New Age. In spiritual warfare, we have countersigns.

The opposition to international recognition of the Queenship of Mary, like the opposition to the new Marian dogma, seems based on the belief that Christians outside the Church might be further alienated by such great honor to Mary at a time when we are seeking Christian unity.

But the encyclical instituting the Feast of Our Lady's Queenship says: "In this doctrine and devotion lies the world's greatest hope." And is not a major part of that hope Christian unity?

We cannot have Christian unity without the fullness of Marian and Eucharistic doctrine. And we cannot have that fullness by hiding our belief.

Let us recall again (it cannot be too often!) that in *Crossing the Threshold of Hope* Pope John Paul II said: "It seems as we approach the millennium, *the words of Our Lady of Fatima are nearing their fulfillment,*" and that we have arrived at the dawn of the 21st century "*in the hope of the definitive coming of the Kingdom of Christ.*"[32]

---

[32] From *Tertio Millennio Adveniente.*

Our Queen's promise of the triumph of Her Heart is a promise of the definitive coming of the kingdom.

The Serpent's Head

Satan unleashed an "all out" attack on the kingdom of God at the dawn of 1800 with the French revolution and the manifesto of Karl Marx. The cathedral of Our Lady in Paris was declared the "Temple to the Goddess of Liberty." A prostitute was enshrined on the main altar.

In counteraction, Pope Pius VII, immediately after his election (1799), crowned a statue of Our Lady as "Queen of the World and Mother of the Church." And a short time later, in that very city (at 140 Rue du Bac), Our Lady appeared as a Queen standing on the globe of the world and *crushing the head of the serpent.*

Then, as Saint Catherine Labouré watched, the vision changed and Our Lady was *holding* the globe (made very small) over Her Heart. She said:

Chapel of the apparitions of the Queen of the World to St. Catherine Labouré. Over the altar, Our Lady stood on the globe crushing Satan. To the right, She appeared holding the globe which She said represented the world and each person in particular.

"THIS GLOBE REPRESENTS THE WORLD and each individual."

At Fatima, She appeared WEARING THE GLOBE (which She held in Her hands in Paris) over Her heart...promising Her ultimate victory. And Pius XII crowned Her there, Queen of the World.

The doctrine and devotion of Our Lady's Queenship, in which Pope Pius XII said "lies the world's greatest hope," *is at the heart of the struggle between The Woman and the serpent.*

Again With Tears

At the very beginning of Her apparition in Paris, standing on the Globe as the Queen of the World and crushing the serpent, Our Lady had tears in Her eyes. She spoke of the chastisements men would bring upon themselves by their sins.

Sixteen years later, She appeared wearing the crown of Queenship on one of the highest peaks of France, at La Salette. Again She was weeping as She spoke of the chastisements men would bring on themselves.

At the dawn of the 19th century (1800), Pius VII crowned Her image, proclaiming Her QUEEN and Mother of the Church. Pope Leo XIII did the same at the beginning of the 20th century. And Pope Pius XII through a legate crowned Our Lady of Fatima QUEEN OF THE WORLD on May 13, 1946.

The Popes have shown us the way from the dawn of the 19th century until now, a time in which we have been in a state of ever more violent spiritual warfare. Our Lady of All Nations, the powerful Queen, will crush Satan when Her subjects respond.

Why We Celebrated the Jubilee

Satan, as Jesus said, is *Prince of this world, the Prince of Darkness.* And Our Lady is the *QUEEN of this world, the Queen of Light.*

Many today recognize the power of Satan through satanic signs.

We have countersigns. The greatest of these are signs of Our Lady and the Eucharist. And foremost among the signs of Our Lady are the Scapular and the Rosary, and another is the crowning of Her images to acknowledge what little Jacinta of Fatima said: "God has entrusted the peace of the world to Her!" We acknowledge, with the Vicars of Her Son, who have named Her Queen, **that *we are Her subjects*, ready to help Her crush the serpent.**

God has determined the triumph will come through Mary. And She has told us at Fatima what to do. If we respond to Her requests, She will crush the serpent and bring about a triumph of love, the triumph of Her Immaculate Heart.

That is why the Pope *commanded* in the encyclical *Ad Caeli Reginam* that on August 22, the Feast of Her Queenship, we renew our consecration to Her Immaculate Heart.

This has been the major theme of my recent book *Now the Woman Shall Conquer* as we look forward to the day when the Pope will proclaim the dogma of Mary as Co-redemptrix, Mediatrix, and Advocate...the last great honor to our Queen in anticipation of Her triumph.

Because of its relevance to all that I have said above and also to what will follow, following are a few paragraphs from that book concerning the prophecies and counsels of Our Lady of All Nations:

She said that Japan would be converted. At that moment Ida (the visionary) felt a stabbing pain in her hand (like the pain experienced by Sr. Agnes at Akita). China, although with great difficulty, will turn towards the Church. ALL nations are to be changed. But Our Lady needs our cooperation in offering the sufferings of Jesus on the Cross.

In the very next apparition at Amsterdam, Our Lady seemed to be looking at Her own hands as She said: *"I see empty hands. I ask you to make known that* **it is my firm determination to form a group from choice people** *who want good and who do good... Much* *time is spent on material things. Let them also spend time on spiritual matters. It is so highly necessary... Let them start to get the younger people back into the right religious mold.*

"Christianity, you do not know the great danger you are in. There is a spirit out to undermine you. But the victory is ours."

The Encyclicals

Over and over again, Our Lady spoke of the encyclicals and of the importance of following them. *Do you know your power? Do you know your teaching?* Then writing the word **ENCYCLICALS,** She added: *Let it flow from right to left, from top to bottom. Do you realize how powerful is this force?... Know well your time has come. This is our time...this means that the Father and the Son now send the Co-redemptrix, Mediatrix, and Advocate over the whole world... They both wish to send the Holy Spirit, Who alone can bring peace.*

Recent encyclicals have elucidated all the most urgent truths of our day, including human life and the Holy Spirit. We have already spoken of the encyclicals on Our Lady as the Woman of the Apocalypse and Queen of the World. *If those encyclicals had been obeyed, we may believe the triumph of the Immaculate Heart, promised at Fatima, would already be here.*

Continuing the messages of Our Lady of All Nations in sequence, She said next:

"I have crushed the snake with my foot. I have been united with the Son, as I am always united with Him. As Co-redemptrix, Mediatrix, and Advocate, I am standing now in this time. The dogma of the Assumption had to precede...

"I have said the world is going to its ruin... With the passing years apostasy and unbelief will set in. The Lady of All Nations stands here and says I want to help them and I am allowed to help them." In the next apparition She said: *"It is high time to unite."*

Chapter Eleven

FEAST OF ST. MARY
GORETTI

On 7/7/96, I had just finished a novena to the little martyr of purity for young girls and women.

M uch of what I have said up to this point, as I have said before, was *in a letter to my sister written within 24 hours after I rose from my "deathbed,"* on July 7, 1996.

The day before was first Saturday. It was also the feast of St. Mary Goretti and I had just finished a novena for young girls and women.

It was not a novena for any particular girls. My heart was aching for all our youth threatened by the modern tidal wave of pornography, contraception, and abortion. And I saw St. Mary Goretti raised to the altar in these days as a much needed, heroic example. In all the ten volumes and thousands of pages of the *Poem of the Man-God,* I can think of only three times Our Lord spoke of contemporary events, and one was the mention of the feast of St. Mary Goretti.

On this very same feast day, some years before, I met her older brother, the one who found her dying from the 14 stab wounds of her martyrdom. Brother Aloysius, whose story is told in that early book *The Brother and I,* had been with me. On that same day, I promised to take Mr. Goretti to Italy to see his sister's shrine. I did, and he died there.

We Had Forgotten it Was Her Feast Day

I was taking Brother Aloysius to the airport. We drove past Mr. Goretti's house. I suddenly slammed on the brakes as I thought that Brother might like to meet the brother of the Saint.

We found him on the side porch. We were visiting with him when an elderly woman walked up the driveway to congratulate him on his sister's feast day.

"By golly," he said, "you remind me! I had forgotten this was her feast." We had forgotten too, because that day a different Mass was said. We marveled at the coincidence.[33] And when Mr. Goretti remarked that he had not seen his sister's shrine (he had not been back since the canonization in 1950 because he could not afford it), I put my arm around him and said: "I am going to Italy a few weeks from now and as *a feast day gift from your sainted sister*, I will take you with me."

It was a particularly touching moment when I drove him to the poor farm south of Naples where he met his younger brother. I was alone as the two hugged each other with tears. Although I had my camera and would have liked a picture to remember the occasion, it seemed too personal and tender a moment for photographs.

He visited other members of his family. When his visit was over, while waiting for the ship in Genoa to return to the States, he died.

This was all so much on my mind the day I did not die that, responding to the supposed mandate of my Heavenly visitors, it was the first thing of which I began to write. And I went on, recalling what had happened the day before.

---

[33] I have often wondered whether this "elderly lady" was an angel. The experience was very unusual.

First Friday

My office is in a two story building near the Blue Army national Shrine of the Immaculate Heart of Mary. I had to prepare the downstairs for the retreat four days later.

Despite my rushed schedule, I decided to go down to the Holy House Chapel to visit the Blessed Sacrament. Our Lord rewarded me. The Shrine sacristan, Joe McCallion, offered to come up and help me move the furniture.

The associate editor of our magazine[34] had called me the night before from Manila to know if it would be proper to use *VOICE* money for travel to do interviews. Since we had been having financial problems, I could not postpone my reply until after the retreat, so I had to squeeze that in. The rest of the day was spent in getting the office ready for the retreat and for the first Friday-first Saturday vigil.

This little building, popularly known as "the red barn," has been the author's office for almost twenty years and the scene of many apostolate decisions. The driveway, uphill, connects to the property of the Handmaids of Mary Immaculate and, downhill, to the national Blue Army center and Shrine of the Immaculate Heart of Mary.

(I do not see the purpose of writing all this. I do so because it was what was happening in my life on 7/7/96. The reader might do well to scan the next few chapters.)

I try to take a nap before a vigil so that I will be sufficiently alert to lead the meditated Rosary, especially the one before the early morning Mass. A dear friend, Marguerite Pierce (niece of the great Cardinal Tisserant), always comes for the vigils. We stopped at the LAF building on the way down to the vigil so I could turn off the chimes of the clock, since Marguerite would be sleeping there. To her great concern, she could not find her keys. Her bag was searched again and again. Then the car. Had she dropped them in the garden? The vigil was about to begin. And I include all these details in tribute to St. Anthony because after praying to him, as though hearing a voice, she reached down in dim light. Her hand came up holding the keys. I often say: St. Anthony has taught many of us the power of prayer by his ready answers to even little ones.

The next piece of trivia is so unusual that if it deserves being printed at all, it deserves being a chapter on its own.

---

[34] *Voice Of The Sacred Hearts*, a magazine sponsored by a group of Philippine Bishops headed by His Eminence Ricardo Cardinal Vidal, founded in cooperation with the International Alliance of the Sacred Hearts.

Chapter Twelve

"REST IN MY ARMS"

*"I believe God is giving us prophets today as
in the past," Rosalie said, "and I feel privileged to
help make their voices heard, so long as they have
approval of a reliable spiritual director, obedient
to the Church."*

As I said, if possible I try to nap before a vigil in
the hope of being more alert. And this Friday
evening prior to 7/7/96, before falling asleep, I
reached for my most-read book, *the Poem of the Man-
God*. It fell open to the story of a man who had been
sent to Ephraim by the Pharisees to kill Jesus.

There is a vivid description of Jesus in a cave on a
stormy night. He has a fire going. Out of the night
comes the murderer, soaking wet, lost, hungry.

Jesus, concealed by His mantle in the dim light,
offers His cloak, His food.

After an amazing dialogue, in which the man (not
knowing that the One offering him warmth and
shelter is Jesus) expresses his conviction that by
killing Him he will be doing a great service to Israel.
Jesus reasons with him and, at a given moment,
stands forth from the shadow and offers Himself to
the poor fellow, whom the Pharisees have brain
washed (just as a few weeks later, He would offer
Himself to the kiss of Judas).

Before the pure love of Jesus, the poor man sees the enormity of his crime. He feels that he is damned. Jesus reaches out and says: **"Come, rest in My Arms."**

Thinking of those beautiful words "Rest in My Arms," I put the book aside and turned out the light. But the thought of resting in the Arms of Jesus was more exciting than soporific. I was too wakeful to sleep so I switched on the light and reached to my bedside table for another book...

This one happened to be a new book given to me by Dr. Rosalie Turton just a few days before. It was written by Carver Alan Ames, an Australian mystic who in just the past few years claimed to have received messages from Our Lord and Our Lady.

I Doubted

I doubted those claims. I was even concerned that Rosalie, whom I greatly esteemed, seemed to accept such things readily.

Without enthusiasm, and expecting the kind of thing one usually reads in these modern alleged messages, I opened it at random. My eyes fell on these words said to have been spoken by Jesus:

*"**Rest in My arms**, rest in My love, rest in Me.*
Live in My arms, live in My love, live in Me.
Pray in My arms, pray in My love, pray in Me."

Those first words were the very words, just read in the Poem, which had prevented me from falling asleep. They were the words of Our Lord to His would-be murderer: "Rest in My arms."

Now it seemed that Jesus Himself was saying those words to ME. I read them over and over. Their wonder refreshed me more than any nap could have done.

That night at the vigil, I gazed at the monstrance with new vision, new feeling (for lack of a better word). I rested in His Arms, in His Love, in HIM. I lived in His Arms, in His Love, in HIM. I prayed in His Arms, in His Love, in HIM.

I remembered an extraordinary thing Dr. Rosalie Turton had told me when she gave me the book just a few days before.

She had arranged speaking tours for various persons and someone called her from Australia asking her to arrange a tour for Mr. Ames. She was told he had apparitions and messages.

"So do others," Rosalie said. "I am sorry but I am not interested."

"He has worked miracles."

"So have others," Rosalie answered.

"But he also has the support of his Archbishop, who appointed a spiritual director whom he sees once a week...*written* approval."

"Well," said Rosalie, "if all that is true, tell him to bi-locate here from Australia and I will arrange a tour for him."

Knock on the Door

To her surprise, shortly afterwards Mr. Ames knocked on Rosalie's door because Jesus had sent him. He was "bi-located" by gifts of persons in Australia who believed so much in him...

Rosalie told me she was rarely so impressed by anyone she has met. (Subsequently she published five books written by Carver and arranged tours for him all over America.)

"I believe God is giving us prophets today as in the past," Rosalie said, "and I feel privileged to help make their voices heard so long as they have approval of a reliable spiritual director, obedient to the Church. And this man is one of them."

But even after Rosalie told me all this, I had not felt like reading words which Mr. Ames said came from Our Lord and Our Lady because there was always, sad to say, *a nagging and persistent doubt that they might be just nice thoughts from his own spirit.* But the doubts vanished when, "at random," (leaving it to the Holy Spirit) I went from the event in the Poem to the words: "Rest in My Arms, rest in My Love, rest in Me..." Now Carver's books are on my waiting list.

That SAME Day!

One reason this episode merits its own chapter is that *on this same day* (first Friday) I read a public condemnation of Rosalie in an official bulletin to all the leaders of the Blue Army in the U.S. because she promoted persons who claimed to have messages from Our Lord and/or Our Lady.

It was heart-piercing to have an organization founded and directed by me for so many years attacking Dr. Turton, probably one of the most sincere and effective lay Catholics I have ever known.

As lay director of the Blue Army I followed a policy not to quote in print any unapproved

Dr. Turton is seen here with a big smile as the last of 940 Peace Flight pilgrims leave the plane singing hymns as they bring the International Pilgrim Virgin into Moscow in October of 1992.

apparition. I even followed this policy in my personal life to such an extent that I missed the opportunity of meeting many mystics of our time, such as Marthe Robin and Theresa Neumann.

But who can deny that God still speaks to us through many voices? There must be many authentic apparitions beyond the very few finally stamped with Church approval.

Although once I printed a warning at the request of a bishop, I would never have thought to suggest that anyone was heretical or disobedient to the church because they believed someone to have had messages or visions. Indeed, if such persons were daily communicants (as is almost always the case), was it likely they would be lying?

I knew Dr. Turton used careful discernment. And she was a person of exceptional personal holiness. I am grateful for 7/7/96 if for no other reason than that it gives me this occasion to defend her since she never defends herself.

As I said, my heart ached to see her attacked and condemned by an apostolate of which I had been a founder. But that was far from the only heartache caused by the apostolate's new direction. That is what had been the major concern of Bishop Hastrich when he died.

Chapter Thirteen

OUR MAIN CONCERN

At the moment, I was especially concerned about the upcoming election to fill positions on the national executive committee, whose nine members ran the apostolate. The apostolate had declined almost overnight from 243,000 militant members to less than 70,000.

B ishop Hastrich and Bishop Venancio, who seemed to be at my "deathbed" on 7/7/96, had played major roles in the history of the Blue Army. If, indeed, they had come to ask me to write "about what you are doing now," would they not want me to write especially of my concerns for the Blue Army?

A few weeks later, there was to be an election to fill three positions on the national executive committee whose nine members ran the apostolate. My concern was that the national delegates (who elect the directors) did not seem to know for whom to vote other than the same directors over and over. I saw little hope of ending the decline, which had taken place in a few short years, from 243,000 militant members to less than 70,000.

This may not seem important to the general reader. However, as Bishop Ahr said: "The Blue Army is important to the Church." Pope John Paul II said in his Oct. 13, 1997 Fatima letter: Fatima is a sign of our times not so much because of the miracle of Oct. 13th, but because it foretells "the later events *conditional upon our response.*" And the Blue Army is the main instrument of that response.

Now Taking a Different Direction

For six years the Blue Army had been emphasizing catechetics (and other broader, general topics) rather than the Blue Army pledge, the Fatima response.

Left to right facing the camera are Bishop Rupp of Paris, the first bishop of Fatima (Dom José Correia da Silva), the Dean of the College of Cardinals (His Eminence, Eugene Cardinal Tisserant), the second bishop of Fatima (Dom Joao Venancio), and Msgr. Harold Colgan (standing). In this historic meeting, almost fifty years ago, Cardinal Tisserant accepted the international statutes of the Blue Army which had been drafted under the direction of the Bishop of Fatima. Two years later, the Cardinal returned in the place of the Pope (as a "legate a latere") to bless the Blue Army international center at Fatima.

The subtitle of *SOUL* Magazine, which for more than 40 years had been *"The Organ of the Blue Army,"* had been changed to *"National Catholic Magazine."* And the overall activities of the entire apostolate (books, leaflets, talks at Shrine events, etc.) reflected this change.

The militant membership, which had developed over a period of *fifty years,* **was evaporating almost over night. Numbers of new Fatima pledges (the primary measure of the vitality of the Blue Army apostolate), after previous annual totals in excess of one hundred thousand, were now in the low hundreds.**[35]

How was I to express my anguish over this great loss? As of the moment of my "heavenly visitors" of 7/7/96, I had decided there was nothing to be done. I had decided on silence. How could I speak without seeming inimical to the good persons who were taking the apostolate in a different direction?

As I was struggling to put this into words, the thought occurred to me that without specific fault-finding it might help to compare the current issue of *SOUL* Magazine (at the moment it was the March/April issue of 1998) with an issue of that same month before the decline of Blue Army membership.

Completely by chance I chose the March/April issue of 1983.

Factual Comparison

In the earlier issue, when *SOUL* had over 200,000 subscribers, the Blue Army is mentioned forty five times. In the same issue of 1998, with less than 70,000, excluding advertisements and a one page

---

[35] All these statistical references are well documented in a professional analysis prepared by James Cash, former marketing executive of AT&T, which was provided to the executive board and all the National delegates at their Fall, 1994 national meeting.

article about the Handmaids of Mary Immaculate, *only ONE mention* of the Blue Army is to be found in all 32 pages of this, the official Blue Army magazine. In the earlier issue, *consecration to Our Lady* (the first element of the Blue Army pledge) was mentioned 49 times.

Before stating how many times it was mentioned in the 1998 issue, please remember that consecration to the Immaculate Heart of Mary is at the very heart of the Fatima message. In his Oct. 13, 1997 letter, the Pope said that at Fatima, God gave us the Immaculate Heart of Mary as our refuge. We fly to that refuge by our consecration, which is made in a quasi-liturgical manner by enrollment in the Scapular. The Blue Army pledge reads: "I will wear this Scapular as a sign of this pledge and of consecration to the Immaculate Heart of Mary."

Wrong Concept

*While "consecration" was mentioned forty nine times in the earlier issue of SOUL, in the 1998 issue it was **not** mentioned even once.*

Most striking is the fact that the one mention of the Blue Army in the 1988 issue was the following single sentence: *"The Blue Army was founded in large part to counter the errors of Russia."*[36]

This was written by the new national director, an exceptional person in many ways, who simply had this wrong view of what the Blue Army is all about.

If one believes the Blue Army was founded in large part to combat the errors of Russia, then indeed its mission might be catechetics. But the Blue Army was NOT AT ALL founded to counter the errors of Russia. It was founded to respond *to the spiritual requests* of Our Lady of Fatima, with a specific pledge

---

[36] In the lead article by the National Director, titled *A Providential Opportunity to Evangelize*, p. 3.

Metuchen Diocese entrusted to Mary's Queenship (see p. 2).

At random we picked out an April issue of SOUL from the past (1983) and compared it to the April issue of 1998. In the old issue the Blue Army was mentioned forty-five times. In the 1998 issue it was mentioned only once, and then, incorrectly.

(Scapular, Rosary, Morning Offering) for the *conversion of* Russia, the *prevention* of annihilation of entire nations, and the "era of peace" following the triumph of the Immaculate Heart of Mary.

None of this is meant to be a personal criticism of the *persons* chosen by the committee elected by the national delegates. It is meant only to point out the drift of the apostolate from its main purpose.

A Helpful Comparison

The difference seen in the change of *SOUL* to a "national Catholic magazine" from "Organ of the Blue Army" might be understood by another comparison: that of general medicine vs. specialized medicine.

General practitioners, who seemed now to be directing the Blue Army, might say: "But the Sacraments are more important" or "Evangelization is more important." And in a sense they are right.

But Our Lady of Fatima has diagnosed for us a specific illness to be treated. It is spiritual lethargy. She said: "So many souls are lost because there is *no one* to pray and make sacrifice for them." *No one seems to care.* Spiritual lethargy has become a destroying cancer. She calls for a radical and specific response. It is a precise prescription to cure lethargy and open the way to the Sacraments.

The Blue Army was founded to administer this remedy.

In our comparison, when *SOUL* magazine became a "national Catholic magazine," the specific remedy, the special prescription given by Our Lady of Fatima to counteract spiritual lethargy, was no longer vigorously applied.

And there has been suffering because of the confrontation between specialist and general practitioner. Such enmity may not occur so often in medicine's struggle to save lives, but Satan makes sure it happens in the struggle to save souls.

Another Comparison

The cancer of spiritual lethargy will be with us even in the coming time of the triumph of the Immaculate Heart. But then the remedy of the Blue Army pledge may be expected to shine forth like the first discovery of antibiotics.

What do we say to those who belittle the Fatima message and the Blue Army Pledge by saying: "It is not *as* important as the Mass and Sacraments."

In reply, we may ask: *"How can we get men and women to daily Mass when many do not go to Sunday Mass, and many who go to Sunday Mass do not go to confession?"*

It is *not* that the Rosary, Scapular and Morning Offering *are more important* than the Sacraments or than Catechetics. But consecration *to our Mother's Immaculate Heart is a first step to holiness.*

The next obvious step is the Rosary. If we can persuade persons to take both steps together (the Scapular and the Rosary), we can be reasonably sure of leading them out of spiritual lethargy. *And when we add the first Saturday devotion, with confession and Communion of reparation once a month, the crawling baby begins to walk in holiness.*

It is not a question of whether the general practitioner is more important than the specialist. Both are important. But for a person too weak to walk, the path to the Sacraments (by which we receive the Life of God) can be opened by the devotions given to us by Our Lady at Fatima. That is why She could promise, if we use those devotions, the triumph of Her Heart, the triumph of God's Love.

My great concern that day I did not die on 7/7/96, believing that Bishop Venancio and Bishop Hastrich with others were are my side, is that while there are many general practitioners, the Blue Army had been the only major specialist applying the prescription given to the nuclear age at Fatima. And now it was failing in its mission.

(Note: Paragraph 67 of Lumen Gentium said that traditional devotions to Our Lady are to be fostered in the Church. *Referring to that paragraph, Pope Paul VI said that the devotions most to be fostered at this time are two: the Rosary and the Scapular of Mt. Carmel.* For a more complete understanding of this very important declaration, please refer to my earlier book *To Prevent This!*).

Division

My protests and urgent warnings against the change of direction in the Blue Army came to be taken as personal attacks on the new directors. And the religious community, which had been founded for the continuity of the apostolate (The Handmaids of Mary Immaculate), was branded as siding with me. The new direction seemed to feel, "It is us or them."

I fell into the trap Satan had set for all of us. By calling attention to the division (in my great concern for what was happening), I seemed only to make it worse. Satan delights in (and is probably the main instigator of) such divisions, even when based, as this one seemed to be, at least in the beginning, on honest differences of opinion.

Effort Made by Bishop Hastrich

To counter the change in direction, Bishop Hastrich persuaded the trustees to appoint Father Richard Bennett as national executive director. He was a wonderful priest who had been deeply involved in our apostolate for many years and was esteemed by both sides. It seemed certain that the division would be healed and that both sides would work together, both for Catechetics and for emphasis on the Blue Army pledge.

But Father Bennett survived this appointment by only one month. He died. And now Bishop Hastrich himself did not have long to live.

To take Father Bennett's place the Bishop now appointed James Cash, an executive recently retired from AT&T and an ardent apostle of the Blue Army and of the Militia of the Immaculate. He had been director of religious education in the nearby Paterson diocese (at times training and directing 80 teachers and 1400 students). In addition to executive experience with AT&T, he had specialized knowledge of building construction. For fifteen years, he had been a volunteer at the Shrine and knew first hand the unique role of the Handmaids in vitalizing the Apostolate and the Shrine. He seemed Heaven sent. But the trustees overrode the Bishop's appointment.

A week later lightning struck the apostolate's main office building. Jim stayed on for three months helping to restore operations and, at this time, made an analysis of the Blue Army's decline with graphs and vital statistics. Most facts cited above are from his report.

Bishop Hastrich greets a wheelchair pilgrim at the Blue Army Shrine.

Crucial Election

With its great loss of membership, the U.S. Blue Army national center now entered a frightening stage of deficit spending, even as much as $300,000 in one year. (There had never been ANY deficit spending in the previous forty years.)

Once again, I do not reveal this to be critical. Were it not for 7/7/96, I would have gone to my grave without ever writing of this in a public manner.

But is not all that has happened perhaps God's way of clarifying the mission of Our Lady's Blue Army?

Out of it all we see an urgent and great need to remind the general Blue Army membership that its delegates to the national meetings bear the ultimate responsibility for the apostolate because they elect the trustees. They should *know each other* so they can vote for those who will see that the Blue Army fulfills its special mission to lead the world to the triumph promised at Fatima, a promise conditioned on the hearing of Our Lady's requests.

Foremost in My Thoughts

This was what was foremost in my thoughts on that 7/7/96. I was going to die. And despite that letter of reassurance Bishop Hastrich had written to me just before he himself died, the apostolate for which I had given my life seemed also dying. And that is not too strong a word. I had been through a similar experience before.

Many think the Blue Army began with the founding of AMI Press and *SOUL* magazine. But it began as a "March of Pledges" in 1946 after my interview with Sister Lucia, the visionary of Fatima. There was also a mandate from the Bishop of Fatima: "Promulgate this as coming from me."

At the time (in 1946), I had a magazine based in New York City with 163,000 subscribers. By 1948, we had over one million signed pledges. Then a new director took over. The magazine became a "National Catholic magazine." The march of pledges was dropped.

Within a few years the magazine not only declined. It died. Publication ceased. The four story office building in New York was put to another use.

But thanks to the inspiration of a wonderful parish priest in Plainfield, NJ (Msgr. Harold Colgan), the "March of Pledges" took on the name he had given it in his own parish: The Blue Army. He and I flew to Fatima and there we buried the million pledges at the

Here, celebrating the 1954 mandate of Pope Pius XII to honor Our Lady as Queen of the World, the Most Rev. Thomas A. Boland, Archbishop of Newark, crowns the International Pilgrim Virgin at a ceremony in Carnegie Hall in New York. Looking on is Monsignor Harold V. Colgan. At left is the first Blue Army banner with the symbol of the Holy Spirit and the Sacred Hearts.

place of the apparitions (beneath the big tree under which the children used to wait for Our Lady). And with purely personal resources, I began all over with the support of my bishop, the Most Rev. George W. Ahr.

We began with the small Catholic publishing company founded in 1940 with the help of my father (a publisher of magazines and newspapers),[37] now renamed AMI Press.[38]

Those who contributed financially were the "militant" members of the Blue Army. They received *SOUL* Magazine, the "voice of the militants."

Heart of the Problem

As was explained above, as of the day I did not die (7/7/96), the problem was not only that *SOUL* had become just another of many general Catholic publications but that it was coming to depend on support by "magazine subscribers" rather than *militant members.*

That in itself could mean the end of the Blue Army apostolate as such. Indeed the Blue Army pledge, that "Fatima formula of holiness," which according to the new constitution is the lifeblood of the apostolate, had previously increased at a rate of up to 100,000 a year. It had now dwindled to a few hundred. Would it soon end?

I had very good reason to fear this because Satan almost brought the Blue Army to a halt more than once before, as told in that history which Bishop Ahr had me write. And now, Bishop Ahr was gone. Bishop Hastrich was gone. Bishop Venancio (the second

---

[37] The Garden State Publishing Co.

[38] It was originally called *The Scapular Press*. The name was now given to the Scapular Apostolate based in New York but the mailing list and other assets of the Scapular Press, which had belonged to me, became the basis of the new Ave Maria Institute (AMI) and the AMI Press.

*The Shrine of the Immaculate Heary of Mary at the U.S.
National Center of the Blue Army.*

bishop of Fatima who had been our major international support) was also gone.

Who was there, outside of the Handmaids and the
veteran Blue Army apostles, who really understood
that while ALL should promote catechetics, our
apostolate was the only one in the world promoting
the Fatima "formula of holiness"—the formula Sister
Lucia had said would bring about the triumph of Our
Lady's Immaculate Heart?

Too Simple

Bishop Venancio often said that a great danger
faced by the Blue Army was that its "formula of
holiness" seemed too simple. The bishop recalled the

incident in the old testament when Elisha the prophet told a leper to wash in the Jordan. But the leper, even though he had come from afar in the hope the prophet would cure him, refused to enter the river. His followers begged him saying that if the prophet had asked him to do something great and difficult ...would he have refused?

The leper was persuaded. He entered the river. He received the miracle.

What Our Lady had told us to do, in order that our world be cured of the leprosy of sin leading us to destruction, is so simple that we can understand how many might think catechetics would be a more important use for the wonderful resources which the Blue Army had developed. Indeed, I was convinced that only persons who really KNEW the power of the Fatima pledge from experience could be sufficiently enthusiastic and dedicated to lead the Blue Army to victory.

Experience Had Convinced Us

We knew not only because of Our Lady's promise but because of a half century of actual experience.

Thousands who made the pledge were "converted" in the deeper sense of conversion. Many became daily communicants. *All night vigils grew in attendance around our nation and around the world.* Padre Pio had said that when as many Catholics had made that pledge as there were Communists, Russia would be converted.

In 1983, one million pledges were signed in the Philippines, adding to more than 25 million of previous years. Only months later at St. Peter's in Rome, the Pope made the collegial consecration and *by the end of that year the collapse of the Soviet Union had begun.*

---

[39] *To Prevent This*, 153 pp., published 1993 by The 101 Foundation, Asbury, NJ, 08802

But I have written of this in many other places, and most recently in my book *You, Too! Go Into My Vineyard!*. And I have explained the importance of the pledge in many other writings. It will all be found in a recent book based on those words spoken by Our Lady at Fatima (after She had said "several entire nations will be annihilated): *To Prevent This!*[39]

The author speaks of this book, written in 1993, as a desperate effort to shake the world by the shoulders and cry: "Now, with continued proliferation of atomic weapons, annihilation of entire nations is possible. But God has sent the Queen of the World to show us how to prevent it!"

Chapter Fourteen

INTERVENTION OF ROME

Unfortunately, the original intention of
the Pope's representative to install a clean slate
of new board members was not followed.

When Pope John Paul II learned of the divisions and the decline of our apostolate, a Bishop was sent by the Vatican to set things right. A new constitution was adopted. The Handmaids were declared to be an "integral" part of the Apostolate. Authority was placed in the hands of an executive committee elected by delegates from all the diocesan divisions.

The original intention of the Pope's representative to install a clean slate of new board members was, unfortunately, not followed. The original committee became self perpetuating.

My concern at the moment (7/7/96), as mentioned before, was that if the national delegates kept on electing the same members, all the wonderful work done by the Bishop sent by Rome would prove to have made little difference.

Father Moreau

Aware of what was happening (through problems which developed simultaneously with our international center in Fatima), Madame Raymonde

The author with Pope John Paul II in April, 1995.

Coquelard, the director of the Blue Army Center in Paris, who had published the French edition of *Dear Bishop*, sent me a copy of Begeron's biography of Fr. Basile Moreau, founder of the Holy Cross order (best known in the U.S. because of Notre Dame University).[40]

I thought I was reading my own story! I went through it over and over (at least four times) hardly able to believe that my own experiences could so closely parallel his, especially when it came to his efforts to save Holy Cross from dissolution...which

---

[40] *Basile Moreau* by Henri-Paul Bergeron, Rome, 1979, 200 pp.

at the end of his life seemed imminent. Bergeron writes:

"Father Moreau set about courageously to bind up the wounds of dissension but difficulties of every kind accumulated through the incessant action of those who sowed discord. He wrote to his community: 'Must we despair of the future?'" (page 152).

When the dissidents had finally gotten rid of him, in a letter of resignation sent to the Pope, he said he was ready to drink the cup to the dregs.[41] Of all the calumnies against him, the most painful was the totally false claim that he had been disobedient to the Holy Father. One of the most common was "misuse of funds."

Yet the year before he died at the age of 74, when he was no longer able to preach because of poor health, he still persevered in his life long custom of fasting and abstaining three days each week, drinking nothing but water, and allowing himself only one full meal a day. For twenty five years a simple armchair had been his bed and his room was unheated. Only shortly before his death did he permit himself to be moved to a heated room with a bed.[42] The strong letters he wrote to those who seemed to be leading Holy Cross to the brink[43] were taken as personal attacks. Only his confessor and a few who knew him well understood to what extent he really loved and forgave those who disagreed with him. They could not understand the agonizing concern of the founder for his threatened child.[44]

---

[41] Original French edition published in Rome, p. 161.

[42] Ibidem, p. 188.

[43] It is largely because of these letters that I identified so much with Fr. Moreau. How many similar letters I had written! And the expressions were almost the same.

One remark of Father Moreau especially struck me. He said the work of a foundation is violently opposed by Satan not only because of its current benefit to souls but because of its possible benefit in years to come. He said that the scars of that spiritual warfare may be seen especially on the founder. To save the foundation, he said, it might even be *necessary* for a founder to be cut off, that he might carry with him all those battle scars, leaving the roots to send forth new shoots.

Father Basile Moreau. Pope Pius XII said in 1945: "Introduce his cause as soon as possible. Devotion to Father Moreau will be a blessing... He is not the only one to have suffered the ingratitude of his own and the wickedness of men."

---

44 These letters of Father Moreau have made his cause for canonization difficult. But Pius XII told the Holy Cross in 1945: "Introduce his cause as soon as possible. Devotion to Father Moreau will be a blessing... He is not the only one to have suffered the ingratitude of his own and the wickedness of men" (Ibidem, p. 197).

Such was the case with Holy Cross. I pray that such may be the case with the Blue Army. The simple formula of holiness given to the world at Fatima was greater than all Her other gifts. It is the very reason why She could promise Her triumph, as Padre Pio indicated in his prophecy: "Russia will be converted when there is a Blue Army member for every Communist." And Sister Lucia, when asked after the consecration whether the annihilation of nations would now be averted, said simply: "The Blue Army will have much to do."

Like Bishop Ahr, Pope John Paul II saw that: "The Blue Army is important to the Church." *There must be an apostolate focused upon dispensing the Fatima formula of holiness until the world is full of saints.*

New Book Just Published in Spain

Fortunately the Apostolate flourishes in many parts of the world, especially where it has a group of religious formed for this purpose to give it continuity.

Banner of the Blue Army of Spain is seen in procession at Fatima on the 75th anniversary of the apparitions, May 13, 1992.

On 7/7/96, a wonderful book had just been published about the Blue Army in Spain where it is the major Marian apostolate, canonically established in all dioceses and recognized by the Episcopal Conference, with a headquarters in Madrid and a beautiful retreat house at Pontevedra at the convent of the First Saturday apparitions. It is staffed by "Blue Army" sisters.[45]

Blue Army Sisters

For more than seven hundred years, the devotion of the Scapular had been entrusted to the Carmelites, the Rosary to the Dominicans, and more recently the Morning Offering to the Jesuits (the Apostleship of Prayer). All three were for the universal Church. But these three communities were given the responsibility to preserve and foster each of the three devotions.

At Fatima, Our Lady holds forth all three together like a "magic formula" of holiness.

This formula, although for the universal Church by the instruction of the first Bishop of Fatima, has been promoted by the Blue Army. *The religious communities founded for the Blue Army have the vocation of fostering the three together, and also the First Saturday communions of reparation.*

A community of more than thirty are at the national Blue Army center of Italy at Turin and in Rome. There are more than forty in the community in Korea.

But the decline of the apostolate in the United States was having worldwide repercussions. The U.S.

---

[45] The religious communities which serve the Blue Army in Spain, and also in Italy and in Korea, are named for the Immaculate Heart of Mary. They are all independent communities but I consider them spiritually one with the Handmaids of the U.S. Blue Army, founded for the U.S. apostolate in 1953.

Blue Army had been the principal support of the international apostolate. The center in Fatima (one of the best pilgrimage facilities there) was defying the new U.S. director, and for more than ten years, no international elections had been held.

This decline was so painful to watch that my wife and I decided in 1996 to move away. But after the Pope's letter of Oct. 13, 1997, we remembered what Lucia had said to Cardinal Vidal when he told her of the success of our *VOICE* magazine (of which I was editor, but with my name absent because of the spiritual warfare):

"Now that we have awakened," she said, speaking of the spiritual warfare, *"it seems that evil is rising.* God will help you and the Virgin will help you... **An army fights... Those who fight win.**"

And so, only by fighting can we win. But, let me get back to the day I did not die!

The Blue Army international center, with byzantine dome, seen from the tower of the Basilica of Fatima.

Chapter Fifteen

THE VIGIL

*Often (indeed, MOST of the time), one is
surprised at the thoughts that come. This
particular night of July 5-6, 1996, it was not
just to keep watch with Jesus...*

I n addition to the basic Blue Army pledge, I had
long believed that First Friday-First Saturday night
vigils could be the final weight on the scales of
God's Justice to save the world from chastisement.
The vigils generously fulfill the wishes of Jesus and
Mary for reparation and for devotion to Their
Hearts...to Their Love. By the vigils, we fulfill the
devotions of both First Friday and first Saturday. We
obtain great graces and almost unbelievable promises
from the Sacred Hearts.[46] Anatol Kaszczuk, the great
Marian apostle of Poland, exclaimed: "Oh, how I look
forward to the first Saturdays when Our Lady reveals
to us the secrets of Her Heart!"

Often (indeed, MOST of the time), one is surprised
at the thoughts that come. This particular night
of July 5-6, 1996, it was not just to keep watch
with Jesus but *quality* time, *heart to heart*. Midnight
began the feast of St. Mary Goretti so there was
frequent reference to reparation and prayer for our

---

[46] See *Night of Love*, a new edition of which was
published by The 101 Foundation in 1997.

young generation, a generation many say has been lost.

"Many souls are lost," Our Lady said at Fatima, "because there is no one to pray and to make sacrifice for them."

In the vigil, united with thousands of others around the world, we were both praying and making sacrifice. We were responding to the call of the Sacred Hearts for reparation. We were offering the sacrifice of this night, and we were praying with all our hearts. We were believing that "nothing is impossible to God," Whose Mother taught us to pray: "Lead ALL souls to Heaven."

The last Rosary of the vigil continued the same theme with increased emphasis on the example of St. Mary Goretti. It was now first Saturday and also her feast day...the day her brother Angelo was visited by myself and Brother Aloyisius and a few weeks later went back to Italy to see her shrine before joining her in Heaven.

Explosion of the Supernatural

I said in the beginning that even if I were to write of all that happened in just the three days of July 5th to 7th, it would take many pages. But there is something else of meaning which happened this same First Friday.

While arranging the office for the upcoming retreat, I came upon the revised manuscript of my book *Explosion of the Supernatural.*

"Glad I found this," I said to Joe McCallion, who was helping me. "One day we should reprint this book."

The following day, first Saturday, I was handed *two very fresh looking copies of the same book* which for some time had been out of print. I could not grasp where they came from. Joe knew.

"Oh," he said, "Dr. Rosalie Turton decided to reprint it."

The day before 7/7/96, the author was suprised to know that this book, which he had intended to reissue "one day," had just been republished.

I was more than just surprised. It must have cost over $20,000. Once again, I had reason to marvel at the initiative and faith of Dr. Turton, an initiative and faith which she backs with fasting and prayer. She never counts the cost and she acts where others hesitate, discuss, often stall in committee. She is not like the turtle that does not move far, keeping its head protected most of the time. Always ready to risk for the glory of God and the salvation of souls, she acts with courageous faith. She exemplifies Catholic Action.

While I wondered in the beginning if all these details of a few days had enough meaning to be recorded, I now realize after recording them that there is. *Explosion of the Supernatural* may mean more in the imminent time of triumph than when it was written. And while I merely thought about reprinting it, someone else did it.

Too Beautiful a Day to Die

Finally let us get past Friday and Saturday. The next day, 7/7/96 was Sunday. And that is always family day.

Almost always on Sunday the family, after Mass, goes for a brunch somewhere. This has been a ritual for years. This particular Sunday the nation was celebrating the postponed July 4th holiday.

The road below the national Blue Army Shrine of the Immaculate Heart of Mary (next to which we live) was the one traveled by George Washington when he retreated from New York. Our nearest principal town is Easton, on the Pennsylvania side of the Delaware River. It is one of only three cities where the declaration of independence was read in the public square in 1776 (the other two being Philadelphia and Trenton).

So, we decided to do something patriotic. We decided to drive through Easton and finally to lunch at the Sun Inn, in Bethlehem, PA., where George Washington once dined.

We had often gone to historic Bethlehem at Christmas or for the music festivals...when there are crowds and crowds of people...happy crowds, busloads from distant places.

Today by contrast, the old town seemed empty and we wandered all over, making an extensive visit to the old Moravian cemetery (many tombs from well before the Declaration of Independence) where many of the Indians who became Christians are buried, including a famous chief. We were steeped in Americana. We were doing something patriotic. And we were together.

In all our years of these weekend outings, I cannot remember EVER when we did not have a "wonderful day." For some reason, this one seemed special.

We walked to the plaza overlooking the "new" city of Bethlehem, the city which made steel famous, or vice versa. From the hill, the tower of one of the Lehigh University buildings seemed to invite us.

The entire university campus goes up, and up, to the very top of the mountain. There we saw a breathtaking view of the Lehigh Valley. We visited the library. The grounds were beautiful. It was another day...in these years of a few weekend hours together...that one felt glad to be alive.

We were home in time for 4:30 p.m. benediction at the Shrine. (There is usually a holy hour at the Shrine every Saturday and Sunday between 3:30 and 4:30, but it had been cancelled today because of a special pilgrimage. It was Haitian day.) The blessing of the "Sacramented" Jesus rounded out the happy hours.

I was glad I had not died today.

I spent the rest of the day writing to my sister...especially about my recent trip to Rome and the conference there on the new dogma.

Chapter Sixteen

HER DOGMA, HER TRIUMPH

*The book picked "at random" proved to
shed a wonderful new light on the dogma of
Our Lady as Co-Redemptrix
and Mediatrix.*

When I went to Rome I was making a sort of spiritual retreat to the extent that I had promised not to watch any television, and to read only spiritual books, for a month.

So the first day I arrived I went to select a book. I entered the great library of the Carmelite Generalate, with its thousands of books, with no one to guide me, and almost without hesitation passed down a very long aisle of tall shelves, around a corner, and reached up and selected a book.

It was written by a Cardinal of whom I had never heard (which is to my shame because he is a great theologian and now on the path to canonization). But I knew *this was the book I was to read.* (Fifty years before, in another Carmelite monastery, I had an almost identical experience leading me to a book which was important to the writing of my first book *Sign of Her Heart.*)

This book proved to be most relevant to the conference which had brought me to Rome, a conference on the proposed dogma of Our Lady as Co-Redemptrix, Mediatrix, and Advocate.

The Big Question

The big question is not whether the Church believes in these titles of Our Lady. The question is whether the faithful should be *bound* to believe in order to be Catholic. And if so, is this the right time to bind them?

Cardinal Gagnon and Cardinal Stickler, two speakers at the conference, agreed with the more than 500 bishops throughout the world who believe that NOW is indeed the time to affirm this belief, even though many others, especially for reasons of ecumenism, hesitate to take the same stand.

Dr. Josef Seifert,[47] who may be considered one of the leading intellectuals in the Church today, began with four difficult questions: Is it not a very serious matter to make belief in Mary's mediation *necessary* to being a Catholic? Is the biblical foundation strong enough? Is this *essential* to Catholic faith? And finally, is it *timely*?

One would like to quote in full the answers to which Dr. Seifert's reason and research led him. In summary, he concluded that the teaching that Mary is Co-redemptrix and Mediatrix IS essential to Catholic faith, there is ample biblical foundation and, furthermore, it is fitting to affirm this NOW when human dignity is assailed. Finally he concluded that we need to affirm *the high role that God has chosen to give to man* for his own salvation, at the heart of which is Mary's fiat.

With the Holy Spirit

I mentioned to one of the principal theologians of the Congress that I had been reading a book about

---

[47] Rector of the International Academy of Philosophy. He has worked directly with the Holy Father in philosophical matters.

the Holy Spirit which indicated *a necessary connection* between the mediation of Our Lady and the action of the Holy Spirit for the triumph of Grace in the world. It seemed not only to confirm the conclusions of Dr. Seifert but to take them to new depths.

"We never thought to focus on the doctrine of Mary's mediation in quite this way," he said with great interest. "It throws a light on the coming triumph of Mary *which will also be the time of the Holy Spirit.*"

The book (to which I seemed to have been directly guided) was written by His Eminence Luis Cardinal Martinez, himself an internationally respected theologian. It was titled simply *El Espiritu Santo.* The Cardinal wrote:

Two Sanctifiers Necessary

Two sanctifiers are necessary to souls, the Holy Spirit and the Virgin Mary, for they are the only ones who can reproduce Christ...

The first is the *sanctifier by essence* because He is God, Infinite Sanctity...and it belongs to Him to communicate to souls the mystery of that sanctity.

The Virgin Mary, for her part, is *the co-operator, the indispensable instrument,* in and by God's design...

These two, then, the Holy Spirit and Mary, are *the indispensable artificers of Jesus, the indispensable sanctifiers of souls.*

Any saint in heaven can co-operate in the sanctification of a soul, but his co-operation is not necessary...while *the co-operation of these two Artisans of Jesus is so necessary that without it, souls are not sanctified* (and this by actual design of Providence).

Age of Mary, Age of Holy Spirit

Cardinal Martinez is giving an existential argument, based on God's own plan for the sanctification of souls. It is not "theory" and perhaps should not even be called an "argument." *It is a statement of reality.* **It is God's plan.**

Holiness is becoming an *alter Christus,* as St. Paul said upon reaching that sublime state to which God calls us all: "I live now not I, but Christ Who lives in me."

And as God willed that Christ come to the world through Mary and the Holy Spirit, He wills that She form Jesus, together with the Holy Spirit, in the mystical Body and in each of us: the Holy Spirit *by His essence,* says Cardinal Martinez, and *Our Lady by Her mediation.*[48]

His Eminence continues: "The Virgin Mary has the efficacious influence of Mediatrix in the most profound and delicate operations of grace in our souls. And, finally, the action of the Holy Spirit and the co-operation of the most holy Virgin Mary are constant; without them, not one single character of Jesus would be traced on our souls, no virtue grow, no gift be developed, no grace increase, no bond of union with God be strengthened in the rich flowering of the spiritual life.

"Such is the place that the Holy Spirit and the Virgin Mary have in the order of sanctification. Therefore, Christian piety should put these two artisans of Christ in their true place, making devotion to them something necessary, profound, and constant.

"The Sanctifier by His Essence...the Virgin Mary the Cooperator, the *indispensable instrument.*"

Holy Spirit and Mary His Spouse

Dr. Mark Miravalle, President of *Vox Populi,* writes: "God the Holy Spirit is the divine Trinitarian member with specific mission of the Father to 'sanctify the Church forever' (cf. Jn 20-22; Rom 15-16; 1 Pet 1...2).[49] But the Holy Spirit has chosen to perform His divine act of sanctification, which flows from the cross of

---

[48] *The Sanctifier,* published by St. Anthony Guild Press, 1957, pp. 6-7.

[49] Also Pope John Paul II, Encyclical letter, *Dominum et Vivificantem,* n. 25

Christ, *only through the mediation of His human but glorified spouse Mary,* through whom the Author of all grace was first mediated to the world by the power of the same Holy Spirit (cf. Lk. 1:35; Mt. 1:18, 20)."[50]

Living in the Divine Will

Cardinal Gagnon said at the 1996 Rome conference: *"It is not enough to believe* that Our Lady is Co-Redemptrix and Mediatrix, we must *proclaim* it." And the Pope affirmed this in his message to the International Mariological Congress later that same year.

Is not the Holy Spirit urging this upon the Church at this time? Are we not speaking of the *reality* of the triumph of the Immaculate Heart of Mary promised at Fatima (*"My Immaculate Heart will triumph"*)...the reality of the forming of Jesus in the Mystical Body and in each of its members to a degree never before attained? And the Blue Army pledge is like a magic formula which opens our hearts to that formation.

An Extraordinary Revelation

At this Rome conference (May 31–June 2, 1996) on the theme of Our Lady as Co-redemptrix, Mediatrix, and Advocate, it was made known that Cardinal Parente had made known the real emphasis the Council had placed on this.

His Eminence had taken part in the actual drafting of Paragraph 67 of *Lumen Gentium,* the principal document of the second Vatican Council, in which four titles are given to Our Lady: Advocate, Helper, Benefactress, and Mediatrix. It was now revealed that these titles were *deliberately placed in ascendance, culminating in the title MEDIATRIX as the crowning*

---

[50] *Mary, Co-Redemptrix, Mediatrix, Advocate* by Mark Miravalle, S.T.D., Queenship Publishing, 1993, p. 52.

doctrine of Our Lady's role in redemption and in the life of the Church.

It struck me that God had permitted that this event of the Council should be made known at just the right moment, just as we had another extraordinary revelation at our seminar of the Two Hearts in Fatima some years before by the Archbishop of Coimbra, who was also on the committee which drafted Paragraph 67.

The Archbishop said that there had been long debate on whether the Council document, in stating that traditional devotions to Our Lady were to be fostered in the Church as heretofore, should mention the Rosary. Finally the committee decided:

"It will be up to the Pope to specify, at any given moment in history, which devotions in particular are to be particularly fostered at that time."

And four weeks after the promulgation of this document, the Pope issued a statement in which he said his thought was in conformity with the Council document and that *the devotions to be particularly fostered at this time were the Scapular of Mount Carmel and the Rosary.*[51]

These are the two devotions held out to the world at Fatima. They are the two devotions of the Blue Army pledge.

I was back from Rome shortly before 7/7/96, the day I thought Heavenly visitors were asking me to write all this. I was glad for at least one reason: There were two thoughts I wanted to share before leaving

---

[51] It seems most Providential that these insights to the drafting of *Lumen Gentium* should come to light. It was on the solemn occasion of the quadrennial International Mariological Congress held four months after the promulgation of *Lumen Gentium* that the Pope declared that the devotions to be fostered, especially at this time, are the Rosary and the Scapular. The actual words of the Pope in making this statement, as in keeping with Para. 67, gives it the aura of Council authority.

this world, and at my advanced age I never thought I would be doing another book through which to share them.

Now that I am about to do so, I am somewhat in awe to find that they illuminate all we have been saying about the new dogma.

*This book, **Now The Woman Shall Conquer**, was just coming off the press on 7/7/96. It includes the messages of Akita and Amsterdam. In the latter, Our Lady said Her triumph would begin with the proclamation of the dogma.*

Chapter Seventeen

THINGS I WANTED TO SAY

*How can Mary be Mediatrix if Jesus is Sole
Mediator? How did Jesus grow in knowledge since
He is God? And is Mary really the
Mother of GOD?*

When I was a young man I had trouble
understanding the St. Grignion de Montfort
devotion and Our Lady's mediation of Grace. A
venerable old Carmelite priest, who looked like a
patriarch and had a reputation for knowledge and
holiness, was kind enough to help me.

"Young man," he said, "I am going to explain
something to you which it took me a lifetime to
understand."

He went on to explain Our Lady's mediation by a
simple example. He said it was as though God, in
communicating Himself to man in the incarnation of
His Son, put in a pipeline from Heaven to the human
race. The end of the pipeline, which is Jesus, was the
Immaculate Heart of Mary. The pipeline was activated
by Her fiat. And after the redemption, for the flow of
Grace, the pipe was *held constantly open by Her fiat.*

They say all comparisons limp. What is really
involved here is not a pipe and a valve, but two
human Hearts used by God to restore man to Divine
Life...two Hearts physically united for nine months,

and even after the birth of Jesus, still united in Love. Saints like John Eudes, Francis de Sales, Jane de Chantal, did not hesitate to speak of the one, single Heart of Jesus and Mary. Abbe Moreau founded the community of the Sisters of the Sacred **Heart** (singular) of Jesus and Mary.[52]

After the analogy of the pipe and valve, I had no more difficulty understanding that while Jesus is the sole Mediator of Grace...the very Pipeline of Grace... Our Lady, the new Eve, is also Mediatrix because, as Dr. Seifert pointed out, *Her fiat,* first required by God 2,000 years ago to undo the sin of Eve, *is still needed at every moment by each one of us.* Such is God's plan, such is His Will.

There are wonderful consequences to this truth.

When we pray to Our Lady, we need not feel that we speak to Her across a sort of chasm between earth and Heaven. She is a part of our "connection" to Heaven. *She is as close to us as God's Grace. She is as close to us as love.*

Venerable little Jacinta said: "Oh, how I wish I could share with all the world my devotion to the Immaculate Heart of Mary!" Too few of us realize the power of this devotion. The Immaculate Heart of Mary is the valve of God's Life to us...life that was lost by the denial of Eve and restored by Her fiat. Does it not follow that the more we are united to Her Immaculate Heart, the closer we are to the Font of Grace?

How Could Jesus Grow in Knowledge?

The second thought I wished to share may answer three questions:

Did you ever find it difficult to understand how Our Lord could grow in wisdom and knowledge

---

[52] *Soeurs du Sacre Coeur de Jesus et Marie.* In 1900 there were over 1,000 in the order, with 154 institutions.

when, as God, He *is* Wisdom and knows all things? Were you ever puzzled that at times He would not know certain things, and at others He knew things He could know only as God? Did you wonder when He said that He did not know the time of the end of the world, that this was known only by His Father?

I always tried to understand by assuring myself over and over that He was at once man and God. But still I wondered how the man, one in the same Person with God, *did not share in all that God knew.*

Then a wonderful example was presented in the person of Blessed Anne Marie Taigi, Patroness of LAF. She was accompanied by a sort of supernatural television set. She was accompanied by an angelic light in which she saw local and world events.

Every time Anne Marie looked into this light she saw happenings present, past, and future. Some were important in the history of the world. A priest appointed by the Pope's secretary regularly came to see her.

Particularly amazing is that in the entire life of Blessed Anne Marie, she looked into that supernatural television set *only when she felt that God wanted to show her something.*

Only when the Father Willed

Our Lord, in His human nature, had a similar Light accompanying Him: the Light of Divinity Itself.

Is it not logical that He permitted His human intellect to look into that Light only when He knew it was His Father's will?

And His Father willed that Jesus be born and develop and grow as *a real man*...that He suffer as a real man...that He even suffer total privation of that Divine Light on the cross, suffering what seemed total abandonment by God. It may be that during all the youth of Our Lord, and often even during His public Life, His Father willed that Jesus should not look into His Divine Light.

The example of Blessed Anne Marie's gift, and how she refrained from using it unless she felt it was what God wanted at that moment, helped me to understand this. It helped me feel closer to Jesus, "man to man" as it were, and to love Him more.

Blessed Anne Marie Taigi was accompanied by a light framed in thorns, in which she saw local and world events. But she looked into the light only when she knew the angel was inviting her to do so.

Each day when we receive Him in His greatest miracle, we may tend to lose awareness of Him as truly man. Understanding that He was and is truly man, while at the same time striving to participate in His relation to the Father, one soars into the almost limitless love of God for us men. And that leads to another question:

The Mother of GOD?

Did you ever wonder how Mary could be the Mother of God since She is a creature of God? Do not mothers exist before their children?

Another saintly Carmelite priest, my own dear uncle[53] who was my guide and mentor during most of my life, explained it this way:

If we look at two women side by side, one a mother and one not, what makes the one a mother is essentially *relationship to a child.*

A mother does not create her child but, in bearing it, the relationship of "mother" is established between herself and this new, other person...her child. And *God established this same relationship between Himself and Mary* by the incarnation and birth of Jesus.

When we look on motherhood *as essentially a relationship,* and remember that Mary became truly the *mother* of the God-Man at the moment of Her fiat, we have no hesitation in saluting Her truly as Mother of God...marveling that God has so honored the human race *by establishing this relationship between Himself and Mary, the new Eve.*

As Dr. Seifert said, this is one of the principal reasons to proclaim the final Marian dogma *now* when the dignity of man is assailed.

Consequences

The greatest saints have been dazzled by this wonder of Our Lady's Divine Maternity. We are told that when the angels were given to know that this was in God's plan, Lucifer's inability to accept such glorification of a human person caused the revolt punished by Hell.

---

[53] The Rev. John J. Haffert, O.Carm., a Carmelite novice master for 27 years. After eight years as a seminarian, and another two years while I was teaching there, I was under his daily direction. See my book *The Brother and I.*

When we say (as we do fifty or fifty-three times in every chaplet of the Rosary) "Mother of God," we are not merely voicing a title. She IS, truly, *Mother* of God.

In a previous chapter, we mentioned that the President of the Pontifical Marian Academy said that the opinion in Rome was that we needed to affirm only that Mary is Mother of God and that all else follows.

This is true. And the consequence of this truth led St. Bernard to say *De Maria numquam satis*, "of Mary, one can never say enough." And St. Augustine said: "She is Queen of the angels because She gave birth to the King of Angels."

In establishing between Himself and Mary the relationship of Mother, God established with Her the relationship of Queen. In the monumental, ten volume work *Somme des Grandeurs de Marie*,[54] Jourdain concludes from the statements of many saints and doctors:

"Almost *endless* would be the texts glorifying the royalty of Mary, relating this royalty to Her Divine Maternity. As mother of the King of Kings, She is *necessarily* Queen and, with Her Son, with a royalty unlimited."

He quotes St. Athanasius who said: "Since He who is born of the virgin is King, in the same manner, and because He is born of Her, this mother who gave Him birth is Queen and Mistress. As She is truly the Mother of God, it is correct to give Her this title."

The more we consider this sublime dignity conferred by God upon Her, creating with Her the real relationship of mother and therefore also of Queen, are we not impelled, as Cardinal Gagnon said, to proclaim **all** Her attributes? Should we not rejoice to call Her also Co-redemptrix, Mediatrix, and Advocate?

---

54 Vol. 1, p. 179.

Chapter Eighteen

ESCAPE FROM JERUSALEM

There was something else I wanted to say
before I died. Now seemed to be the
most appropriate moment.

S t. Alphonsus was in his nineties when he said to
the companion reading to him: "My, what a
wonderful book! Who wrote it?" It was his own
Glories of Mary.

Some readers might have thought he was guilty of
self promotion when, in the preface of another book,
he did not hesitate to say that *he hoped everyone would
read it.*

But a book with a heavenly message has something
objective, something which the author is likely to
perceive as outside himself. And the heavenly
message is certainly one the author wishes *everyone*
would read.

I had no intention of writing this book. Indeed
writing books, although I have written more than
twenty, was not my main vocation. I wrote far more
in magazine articles over the years. My vocation was
simply to promote the message of Fatima.

But I do not hesitate to say of most of the books I
have written that I wish, indeed I pray, that if not
everyone at least *many* will read them. And I have no
self interest. I offered them all to Our Lady. Any

income from any of them has gone to the apostolate, and will continue to do so.

Time of Disbelief

I bring up this subject because recently we have been hearing of "great" theologians who use high sounding words and erudite style to deny transubstantiation. And since I hope at least many lay apostles may read this present book, I want to urge them to read and diffuse *The World's Greatest Secret.*

I wrote it in the hope of introducing Protestants and non believers to the "believability" of the true presence of Our Lord in the Eucharist, never thinking that it might one day be a book greatly needed by Catholics. Indeed, I never dreamed that in my lifetime there could be such apostasy and veiled heresy as now. When I heard that more than half of the Catholics in the developed countries no longer believe in the true presence, I thought it must be a diabolical exaggeration.

As I submitted this present book in advance to about two dozen selected critics, I submitted the book on the Eucharist to hundreds. And it is interesting that one doctor of theology commented:

"It will succeed... It is based on facts, not clouded by diverse opinions..."

The fact is that the wonder of the Eucharist was so important and so sacred that it was indeed the greatest secret in the history of the world...a secret to be revealed only to those who had been carefully prepared to share it.

When I began the book in the early sixties, wonderful archaeological discoveries were being made around the Mediterranean, and by a Providential "accident," the tomb of the first apostle was discovered deep beneath the dome of St. Peter's. That gave me the idea of writing this basic book on the Eucharist (which is the heart of the Fatima message) by beginning in the catacombs.

I had seen the need for such a book during most of my life but never discovered the angle from which to start, until a workman digging in the floor of St. Peter's crypt fell into that first century cemetery.

Many Offer Prayer Support

But I felt so unworthy of writing on a subject so sublime...the subject of the greatest of all God's acts of love after the Incarnation, and the subject of Our Lord's greatest miracle. I trembled at the thought. No such book had, to my knowledge, ever been written.

But if Our Lady could make known the true presence of God in the Eucharist to the children of Fatima in one flash of light from Her Immaculate Heart, could not the world hope for that light?

I decided to start a private campaign of prayer which would last until the book was finished. I took advantage of contact with many holy souls in the Fatima apostolate. One by one, I enlisted pledges of prayer support. Ultimately I had over two hundred devout souls who promised to remember this intention in their *daily* Communion.

Little did any of us know that it would take several years.

I rented an apartment in Rome and worked there off and on until 1965. A trial edition came out in 1966. When the final edition appeared a year later, I felt confident the prayers had been heard.

Praise from Protestants

The most Reverend F. Pierce Corson, former president of the World Methodist Council, said: "It should help *all* to understand." A Jewish reader said: "I couldn't put it down, and for the first time I understood what Christians believe..." An Anglican reader in Edmonton, Alberta, said: "I felt I was in another world... I do not think I have ever read a book that lifted me so much, other than the bible."

Remarks of Catholics were expected to be favorable and I was gratified by comments like those of Cardinal Cushing of Boston who said it was "tremendously needed," and Cardinal O'Boyle of Washington who said it was "timely and important." But greatest satisfaction came from the reaction of non Catholics and especially the day I learned that a Muslim doctor, after reading this book, believed in transubstantiation and became a Catholic...and wrote a book in the hope of converting other Muslims!

It is a book not just for those initiated solemnly to the revelation of the secret but *for everyone.*

Among the "saints" from whom I solicited prayers for this almost impossible task was Padre Pio. I had gone to Italy to see him several times and even had the grace to serve his Mass. I considered him one of the world's greatest witnesses to the True Presence.

He never said yes or no to my requests for spiritual help with the book. Each time I asked, he

*Padre Pio was a primary inspiration for the author's book on the Eucharist: **The World's Greatest Secret.***

just looked at me. I sometimes wonder whether it was because he wanted me to pray more, to ask more, to rely more on supernatural help. And then one day, after the book was printed and had already sold over 100,000 copies, a priest, to whom Padre Pio confided, told me:

"Padre Pio said it will have some success while you are alive, but its greatest success will be after your death."

So it seems fitting now, as this is published after the 7/7/96 experience and in my 83rd annual step to the day I shall surely die, that I write of this.

A Special Sign

One of the special signs, or "lights," in the course of writing *The World's Greatest Secret* happened two days before the six day war in Palestine, in 1967.

I had come to Jerusalem with a group of pilgrims to pray for the successful conclusion of the book...specifically to be there on Holy Thursday when we would pray on that very day in the upper room, the site of the last Supper...the place where the world first heard those amazing words: *"This is My Body."*

No one announces when a war is about to begin. Japan did not send advance notice of its attack on Pearl Harbor, and Hitler did not send out notices of his march into Poland. I just "felt" that a war was about to begin. And our group was right next to the wall which separated Arab Jerusalem and Israel.

Despite our great desire to be in the cenacle on Holy Thursday, I firmly announced to the group that we were leaving.

They were incredulous. I told those who objected to stay if they wished, but that I felt the group to be in danger and I would leave with all who agreed.

Fortunately all did. When we arrived at the airport, the plane was held up because the U.S. consul and his wife arrived at the last moment. They had just been advised and left so hurriedly that their food was still on the stove in the consulate kitchen.

Less than 48 hours later the building in which our group had been staying was gone.

What Did Our Lord Plan For Us?

The only plane we could get was to Beirut, where we had to wait a few days for ongoing transportation.

Why had all this happened? Why were we suddenly in Lebanon? Was there any special shrine, any special holy place we might visit for that ultra special day: Holy Thursday?

Someone said: "There is a tomb up in the mountains to the north of Beirut of a very holy man. Many go there because of miracles."

We had never heard of the holy man, a Maronite priest by the name of Charbel. But the feeling came: *"That is where you should be on Holy Thursday."*

The group agreed and we hired cars and climbed up thousands of feet to that remote monastery without knowing why.

When we arrived in early morning to have Mass, we were led to the tomb of Father Charbel, as though it was presumed that was why we came. Mass was about to begin when I suddenly realized we did not know why we were there.

Mass was delayed while I went off to find one of the monks to ask: "Do you have a book or pamphlet about Fr. Charbel we might read at our Mass?"

Great Witness to the Eucharistic Miracle

The one he gave me was over a hundred pages. Our chaplain was vested. The group was waiting. We opened the book and read "at random"...as the Holy Spirit directed.

The book fell open to a description of Father Charbel's life-focus *on the Mass and the Blessed Sacrament.*

Alhough the priests of his community went out to serve in parishes, as part of their religious life they had a hermitage where individual priests might go to make private retreats...usually for a few days at a time.

Fr. Charbel began by extending the few days of hermitage to a few weeks, and finally he had permission to remain in the hermitage concentrating his entire life around the Holy Sacrifice. He slept only four hours. The rest of the time was spent preparing for Mass, saying Mass (which took him about three hours), and making his thanksgiving.

The very place were I opened the book spoke of the death of Fr. Charbe,l which began while he was saying Mass. *He was holding up the consecrated Host and praying almost the very words taught by the angel to the children of Fatima: "O Most Holy Trinity, I offer Thee the Body, Blood, Soul, and Divinity of Jesus Christ, in reparation for the outrages, sacrileges, and indifference by which He is offended. By the infinite merits of the Sacred Heart of Jesus and the Immaculate Heart of Mary, I beg the conversion of poor sinners."*

A monk assisting at the Mass thought Fr. Charbel was taking a bit longer time holding up the Host. But after almost half an hour passed, he thought he had better call the old hermit out of his ecstasy.

To his amazement, Father Charbel, clutching the Sacred Host, was paralyzed in that position. The Host had to be forcefully removed. Father Charbel was laid on the floor behind the altar where he finally died.

Difference of Rites

At once the reader may wonder, when Latin Masses may last as few as twenty minutes, how Father Charbel could take three hours to say Mass, and how he could pray what seemed to be his own prayers after the consecration.

The reason is primarily because Father Charbel was a priest of the Maronite rite, which is quite different from the Latin rite. Another reason is because he had permission.

Father Pio used to take two hours to say Mass...just the basic Mass, with no homily. Most of the time seemed just before, during, and after the consecration. (Later, because of complaints from some of his critics, Fr. Pio was put under obedience to take no more than an hour, and from the time of that obedience his Mass was never longer.)

Calvary Really Present

Padre Pio began to suffer even before he left the sanctuary. He was about to be present on Calvary and the very real wounds in his hands, his feet, and his side were more painful than usual. I had the privilege of serving his Mass, and during one of those long Masses I could read the missal. I saw how he suffered at the consecration. Truly, the Mass made Calvary present.

He could barely pronounce the words of consecration. Over and over he gasped out the sound of the "h" before finally pronouncing the word "Hic." Then followed a time in which he seemed to gather strength before a great effort to pronounce the next syllable...

Again he gasped the initial sound over and over before finally, almost explosively, he said "est." And so it went on until finally he had completed with the words "Corpus Meum." And the agony went on until Jesus had taken the place of the substance of both the bread and the wine.

The Sign of a Eucharistic Priest

I happened to be in Rome years after that unplanned visit to Beirut. I was making a usual visit to St. Peter's and I was surprised to be greeted by a Maronite priest I knew from the States. "Oh," he said, "how wonderful *you came for the beatification of Father Charbel!*"

I was taken completely by surprise. I had not known. Had Father Charbel, that great living witness of the True Presence, drawn me again? Was I to be a witness to this great witness of the Mass and the Eucharist?

I did tell his story at least briefly in *The World's Greatest Secret*. I hope that many more will hear about Father Charbel, of the miracle of his incorrupt body, and that now he is a canonized saint. Witness like his and that of Padre Pio can drown out the dissident voices.[55]

There are so many things we do not know... In my lifetime, with the advantage of being multilingual, I have read hundreds of books. And the more I learn the more I realize I do not know.

But one thing we are coming to know beyond all doubt. The laity must participate *actively* in safeguarding our devotion and faith in the Eucharist.

This is also the command of the Council and of the magisterium.

In *Tertio Millennio Adveniente*, we read in Para. 37: "There is need *to foster the recognition of heroic men and women* who have lived their Christian vocation in marriage. Precisely because we are convinced of the abundant fruits of holiness in the marriage state, we need to find the most appropriate means for *presenting them to the whole Church* as models and encouragement."

---

[55] While *The World's Greatest Secret* was written with non-Catholics in mind as well as Catholics, there is a new book for Catholics already living a Eucharistic life which we strongly recommend as one of the very best: *Mary and the Eucharist* by Fr. Richard Foley, S.J., 195 pp., published in 1998. Available from LAF or from P.O. Box 308, Newtonsville, OH, 45158-0308.

Chapter Nineteen

"MOBILIZE THE LAITY"

*For hundreds of years the role of the laity
in the life of the Church was under emphasized.
Before the apparitions of Our Lady of All Nations,
only one adult layman (Bl. Benedict Joseph Labré),
other than political figures or martyrs, had
been canonized in over 500 years.*

Having been a lay apostle almost by profession for over fifty years, and now no longer occupied with the direction of the Blue Army, in 1995 I wrote the book *You, Too! Go Into My Vineyard!* and started the Lay Apostolate Foundation.

Dr. Tom Petrisko,[56] in my opinion one of the truly great lay apostles in the U.S., recently called me to say that he had been given new light on the role of the laity in the work of the Church and was producing an 18 page "newspaper" on the call of the laity to holiness, to be distributed by the millions. *"I believe God withdrew you from the Blue Army,"* he

---

[56] Dr. Petrisko is author of several books and producer of "newspapers" on religious subjects distributed by the million. His latest is on lay saints— the call of the laity to holiness. Contact: *Center for Peace*, 6111 Steubenville Pike, McKees Rock, PA, 15136. Tel: 412-787-9791. Fax: 412-787-5204.

said, *"in order to start the Lay Apostolate Foundation. This will be the most important work you have ever done."*

(Incidentally, Dr. Petrisko had also published a multimillion edition of a newspaper on the Eucharist in which he promoted *The World's Greatest Secret.* I thought at the time: "He will be the one to make Padre Pio's prophecy come true!")

Providential Persons

At first I thought the Lay Apostolate Foundation would begin to function fully only after my death. But a meeting of the board just a few months before 7/7/96 confirmed officers, finalized the constitution and bylaws, and voted to hold a retreat involving some of the most outstanding lay apostles of our time the following July 12–17th (five days after 7/7/96).

Just setting up the Foundation had been a major task. I was helped in the beginning especially by Dr. Rosalie Turton of the 101 Foundation, Father Richard Soulliere of the Archdiocese of Miami (Director of Marian Movements of the Archdiocese and Spiritual Director of the Archdiocesan Council of the Legion of Mary, which has jurisdiction over five Southeastern States), and by Julia Ceravolo, who had produced a series of excellent Catholic TV programs which were shown on EWTN and on the Bishops' network.

For the celebration of the golden jubilee of the Queenship of Mary, we decided to invite the Marian Shrines throughout the world to participate in an international *television program* on the Queenship of Mary. With Julia's consent, GEM Productions became CATHOLIC TELEVISION (LAF), and in this name the invitations were sent to Marian Shrines throughout the world. The final program was all put together under the direction of Howard Dee in Manila.

Long Overdue

Unfortunately, for hundreds of years the importance of the role of the laity in the life of the Church had not been sufficiently recognized. Before Vatican II *only one adult lay person,* other than political figures or martyrs, had *been canonized in over five hundred years.*

One of the goals of LAF is to make known lay models of holiness, many of whom are coming to the fore since the Council.

In keeping with the message of the Council and the importance he himself had put upon this, Pope John Paul II told the Congregation for the Causes of Saints to concentrate on causes of the laity so we would have models and exemplars of holiness in the lay state. By joyous coincidence, the very day we celebrated the Golden Jubilee of the coronation of Our Lady of Fatima as Queen of the World (Aug. 22, 1996), Frederick Ozanam was beatified. (Read his wonderful story *The Apostle with the Top Hat,* available from LAF or The 101 Foundation.)

The home of St. Benedict Joseph Labré in Amettes, France. He left to enter a monastery, but after several tries he finally realized his vocation was in the world. His greatest devotions were to Our Lady and the Eucharist. In Rome, he was known as "the man of the forty hours," because he went day after day to the churches where the forty hours devotion was being held.

Like Frank Sheed and Maisie Ward of our century, Blessed Ozanam began to defend the faith on street corners.

It was a time of great distress and poverty after the French revolution. The atheists challenged him: "What did the Church do for *les misérables*?" How was Frederick to respond?

Instead of using only words, at the age of only twenty, he founded the St. Vincent de Paul Society. Today 880,000 members serve the poor and aged in every part of the world from 46,650 centers.

Frederick was born into Heaven on the birthday of Our Lady, Sept. 8, 1853. He was only 40 years old. He was survived by a wife and daughter...*and millions of lay apostles of these past 130 years.*

Five days after 7/7/96, and six weeks before the Queenship Feast and the beatification of Ozanam, we held our first Lay Saints Retreat.

Successful Beyond Expectation

The first retreat gave voice to no less than a dozen different apostolates. In the discussion periods, as we mentioned before, the leaders addressed the question of a possible chastisement. They unanimously agreed that it could be avoided, or at least mitigated, if the spirit evidenced in this retreat could prevail.

The following year the theme was taken from the words of Our Lady of All Nations: "Mobilize the Laity." Leaders of apostolates from the U.S., Ireland, England, and Australia participated. We not only discussed the mandate of Our Lady of All Nations, we experienced it. The enthusiasm generated by this getting together of apostles far exceeded anything we had hoped or envisioned.

To make known lay models of holiness, as requested by the Pope, LAF has already published leaflets on the lives of several. Among them is Blessed Isidore Bakanja, who could be called a martyr of the Fatima pledge. Not only did the Scapular and the

Rosary help to make him a saint, but they were the specific occasion of his martyrdom.

Models of Holiness in the Laity

When *Inside the Vatican* reported efforts to remove Pope John Paul II, LAF held up the example of lay saints who in the past came to the aid of the papacy: St. Nicholas of Flue, St. Catherine of Siena (a Third Order Dominican), Bl. Elizabeth Mora, and Bl. Anne Marie Taigi. Ultimately well over a million leaflets were distributed in the English speaking world alone. It was also widely distributed in other countries.

So the Lay Apostolate Foundation was becoming an instrument of various activities surrounding its main purpose: to respond to the command of Our Lady of All Nations, *"mobilize the laity."*

Blessed Isidore Bakanja became a Christian as a teenager. The Rosary and Scapular were his formula of holiness. He was mercilessly scourged by an atheist employer because he would not remove his Scapular. He died Aug. 15, 1909, Rosary in hand and the Scapular around his neck. He was beatified in 1995.

Chapter Twenty

THE LAY APOSTOLATE
FOUNDATION

*Marthe Robin, who lived the last 30 years
of her life solely on the Blessed Sacrament, said
that the laity will save the Church. She called for
the five day retreat. LAF is a response to her
example and message.*

The continuity of the Blue Army in it's pristine fervor, as I said in the beginning, was still a major preoccupation on the day I didn't die, as it had been for fifty years.

After the basic Blue Army pledge (necessary to obtain Our Lady's promise) was no longer vigorously promoted, there seemed little I could do. So, following the 1992 Peace Flight to Russia, I inaugurated the magazine *VOICE OF THE SACRED HEARTS* to promote the pledge once again, together with the First Saturday Communions of reparation.

On the day I didn't die, this was my major occupation.

*As the Pope pointed out in his Oct. 13, 1997 letter to Fatima, what is most important about Fatima is the **response** to Our Lady's requests.* And following the change in Russia there was added stress on the first Saturday Communions of reparation.

Our Lord had insisted that the consecration of Russia to the Immaculate Heart of Mary be made by all the bishops of the world because: *"I want all the world to know* that it is through Her that this favor (the change in Russia) is obtained, so that **afterwards** *devotion to Her Immaculate Heart will be placed alongside devotion to My Own Sacred Heart."*

And *now* was *afterwards.*

Immediately following the collegial consecration on March 25, 1984 we had the change in Russia. We had the sign Our Lord gave "so all the Church will know." *But His subsequent request, regarding first Saturday devotion, was largely ignored.*

So I suppose if asked what I was "doing" on 7/7/96, I would have said I was editing this magazine—promoting the "pledge" to fulfill the requests of Our Lady of Fatima with new emphasis on the first Saturdays.

The entire first issue of the magazine was translated and delivered to Sister Lucia. The following October 11, 1993, the year after the magazine began, Cardinal Vidal asked her in a personal interview whether this apostolate fulfilled Our Lady's requests.

"I believe it does," she answered, "because *this movement shows itself to be the fulfillment of what the Virgin spoke* to promote the Communion of reparation, which is the means to combat atheism... *The Virgin is interested in everything (the entire pledge)* but particularly in the Communion of reparation."[57]

---

[57]At the time, the author played an important part in this "movement" (to which Sister Lucia refers) as editor of *VOICE* magazine. Within four weeks of this interview, in which Sister Lucia also referred to the efforts of Satan to destroy it (of which we have spoken elsewhere), Cardinal Vidal wrote to the author: "You are indeed a brave apostle of Mama Mary. We hope that our partnership in the apostolate of the Two Hearts will remain forever."

This January 1996 issue of **VOICE OF THE SACRED HEARTS** *shows Cardinal Vidal presenting to the Holy Father a book of theological–pastoral resolutions of the Alliance of the Two Hearts seminars held throughout the world. In his right hand, His Eminence hold the special issue of* **VOICE,** *shown on pg. 6, of which Haffert was editor and of which he says: "On the day I didn't die, this was my major occupation." Sister Lucia had told the Cardinal on October 11, 1993 that this apostolate was* **"the fulfillment of what the Virgin spoke..."**

A Burden Lifted

Because of the magazine, I had to squeeze in other work, including my continuing concern for the Blue Army and especially a new work I had begun: The Lay Apostolate Foundation. Involvement of the laity in the life of the Church had been the most innovative message of the Second Vatican Council. It had also recently been the subject of a book-length exhortation by the Pope: *Christi Fideles Laici*... And, as I said before, having been a layman involved in the life of the Church for over half a century, I felt I might help others follow the path now delineated by the Council and by the extraordinary exhortation of the Pope.

Soon after 7/7/96, the Philippine group sponsoring the magazine opened a U.S. office staffed with full time dedicated personnel (much like *Donum Dei*). They felt able to take over the magazine entirely before the end of the year (1996). I rejoiced that the apostolate of enthronement of the Sacred Hearts in homes, with emphasis on holiness in families and on the First Friday/First Saturday vigils and Communions of reparation, was rapidly reaching out to all the English speaking world and beyond. And the quality of the magazine, although it came out at somewhat irregular times, continued. I am proud to have had a part in it.

Now I had more time to devote to the Lay Apostolate Foundation which I now considered *my major "end of life" work.*

Structure

To begin the Foundation, I expected to use money from a life insurance policy, which Msgr. Colgan and the Blue Army trustees had set up for me many years before (because I was accepting no more than a subsistence salary). When I did not receive it from the new direction, I was afraid, because I knew I had not many years to live, that LAF might not materialize. Then a stock in our trust fund skyrocketed. The windfall enabled us to start the Foundation. (Ultimately the entire trust will be used to perpetuate it.)

The most I had hoped to accomplish, in the few years of vitality left to me, was to structure the Foundation. I began by writing the book *You, Too! Go into My Vineyard!*. Then, with the help of the gifted and very dedicated persons already mentioned, four years later (only five months before 7/7/96), a Council of selected laity and clergy was chosen to determine the policies of the Foundation, with nine officers elected to staggered three year terms.

Any officer of this Council, after two or more terms, may be elected to the Board of Directors which controls the funds and carries out the mandates of the Council. In the event of inability or objection to the carrying out of any given mandate, said mandate may be voted upon again at the next meeting of the Council.

Check and Balance

This may seem very simple. But the problem was to provide what may be called "check and balance." That is why the Directors, who are elected for life, are given the right to postpone implementation of a project and have it submitted to a second vote.

We gave similar balance to the Blue Army by making the Handmaids (the Blue Army Sisters, with their vow of poverty and their unquestioned dedication and integrity) trustees. Only they could sign checks. But under the new direction, new signatories were assigned to the bank accounts and the executive committee itself became the trustees.

There followed expenditures not brought to the attention of the Blue Army National Council. Even information about salaries, to which members of the Council were entitled, was withheld. Under the new direction, at one national meeting after another, no financial statement was released to the national membership. At the 1997 meeting, the delegates were told that great progress was being made because the previous year the deficit had been $300,000 and this year it was only $50,000. End of financial statement. As I said before, I mention this not in criticism but to point out the need for the general Blue Army members to be informed and to vote responsibly.

But getting back to LAF, which I hoped would have a sound structure for the future:

In 1977 a mailing was made to 2,000 selected persons asking if they would be interested in participating in LAF. From 1,200, who responded in the affirmative, we selected the LAF Council.

I had always seen the need for lay formation. Some of our best Blue Army apostles were from the "schools" of apostolic formation which we conducted, especially in that famous period of the "sixties," in the U.S. and in Fatima.

One of our models in this was Frank Sheed who, with his wife Maisie, were stars of the Catholic Evidence Guild. Frank said: "It took a tremendous amount of training... We asked people to come for classes two nights a week. We left no point in Catholic theology untouched. That course took from two or three years to master. Even after that, we put them in touch with individual theologians who looked after their further development."[58]

Formation of Daily Communion

We do not expect a five day retreat to do all this. *But there are a surprising number of devout laity already well informed.* Our questionnaire revealed that *many daily communicants read Catholic books extensively, and*

---

[58] From interview with Frank Sheed which appeared in *New Covenant* magazine, Vol. 11, Number 2, 1981. Catholic Evidence Guild, Ann Arbor, Michigan, 313-995 3125.

some exclusively. And we learned that *many* daily communicants today are aware of the critical need for their involvement in the life of the Church. Many have told us that, feeling the need to be active, they have longed for just what LAF is doing.

My brief experience has shown that long time daily communicants have already been formed by Jesus Himself as they have received Him day after day. In his book *The Church and I,* Frank Sheed makes the same observation. And LAF hopes not only to encourage them but *to put them in touch with each other* and with the growing expansion of lay involvement in the life of the Church. Publications, videos, retreats, and personal contacts are some of the ways to make this possible.

Is this not at least part of what Our Lady of All Nations was telling us to do when She said that we must now mobilize the laity?

Current Projects

Shortly after 7/7/96, I translated into English an old French version of the life of St. Benedict Joseph Labré, which is to be published by the Benedict Joseph Labré Guild, a recent and much needed apostolate for millions of mentally ill and the more millions of the families affected by drug addiction and mental illness.

LAF NEWS is sent periodically to all the Councilors and supporters to report the activities of the Foundation and of various lay apostolates multiplying under the powerful force of the Holy Spirit throughout our nation and throughout the world.

Perhaps we can sum it all up again by recalling that Marthe Robin, who lived the last 30 years of her life solely on the Blessed Sacrament, said that the laity will save the Church. She called for the five day retreat. LAF is a response to her example and message.

Chapter Twenty-One

NOW! (TWO NEW BOOKS)

Two books were just coming off the press on 7/7/96: NOW THE WOMAN SHALL CONQUER, and NIGHT OF LOVE.

On 7/7/96, I had two books just about to be released. They were the final two of the last books I had long felt compelled to write, but for which I had not found time while director of the Blue Army and editor of *SOUL* magazine.

The first of these "last" books was *Her Own Words to the Nuclear Age.*

Most Important Book

This was a book **with a message from Heaven**

1) **written by the person** who, in that message from Heaven, was **left on this earth to write it;**

2) **containing a secret** so grave that four Popes in succession agreed not to make it public, but which **is made public NOW;**

3) promises an **era of peace for mankind,** but only after **several entire nations will be annihilated** unless this message is heard;

4) is specifically **addressed to the nuclear age with seven major prophecies,** all of which have come true except two, and those two **affect every man, woman and child on the planet.**

Since I really believed all this, the reader may wonder why I waited until God saw fit to bump me out of the direction of the Blue Army before writing it.

Part of the answer is that I trembled before the responsibility.

From the time I first interviewed Sister Lucia in 1946, and became a personal confidant of the first two bishops of Fatima, the need to write this weighed upon me. The second bishop, the Most Rev. John Venancio, looked on me as one of the major experts on Fatima, and that added to my sense of responsibility.

So this particular book, although it took only a few months to put on paper, was fifty years in the making in my mind and in my heart. All through those fifty years, I had gathered knowledge and experience. But I still worried about my ability to *convince* readers of what Sister Lucia told me: *Specifically what was needed to save the world from nuclear war* contained *in a simple "pledge" which was finally signed by over twenty five million in more than a hundred countries,* **and without bloodshed, the Soviet Union was dissolved.**

Now we were at the final phase. We were at the dawn of a new era...and we had the choice of entering it by Grace alone or by Grace and fire. Entering the third millennium, the need to respond to this message from Heaven had become more urgent than ever.

How could any words of any writer adequately meet the need?

The urgency was emphasized by the Holy Father in a special letter to Fatima for the 80th anniversary of the miracle (Oct. 13, 1997), which I have quoted repeatedly in this present book. His Holiness said that the miracle was one of the *greatest signs of our times,* not only because of the miracle itself but because of the ALTERNATIVE it offered. He said that at Fatima God has given us, in the Immaculate Heart of Mary, a *refuge.* "From Fatima She spreads Her mantle over the world," the Pope said. And he called again, as he had so often before, for a worldwide response.

I was much encouraged by Joseph P. Barrett, a professional journalist with one of the nation's major newspapers, who said:

"I wanted to get the latest and overall picture of Fatima, so I decided to read Haffert's *Her Own Words to the Nuclear Age.* As I read the book, what came to me was: The Holy Spirit inspired this, just as He inspired Lucia as she wrote her diary. I could hardly put it down."

Authentic

The official documentarian of Fatima was the internationally known theologian, Dr. Joachim Alonso, whose complete documentation on Fatima fills *eighteen volumes.* It was he who personally urged me to produce *Her Own Words to the Nuclear Age* and confided to me his own personal notes. And it was with Bishop Venancio and Dr. Alonso that we arranged to turn the convent of the last apparitions (at Pontevedra, Spain) into an international shrine. So, there was also personal witness to be given.

Even though somewhat consoled by comments like those of journalist Joe Barrett, I feel that I have been a failure, or at best only slightly successful, in making known the URGENCY of responding to the Fatima alternative. The airline, which had taken 22,000 pilgrims to Fatima in one year, was no longer flying. The major film we had produced at the cost of $5 million had not been released.[59] I had never really

---

[59] The airline SKYSTAR was founded to provide a special plane dedicated to Our Lady as Queen of the World. It flew directly from airports all over the U.S. directly to Portugal. It ceased operation after the terrorist attack at Rome airport, which caused the failure of several overseas airlines, crippling even giants like Pan American and TWA. The film will be mentioned in a later chapter.

succeeded in shaking the whole world by the shoulders and saying: "NOW is the time!"

I wrote *Now*[60] almost as a last desperate effort. It was an update of all of Our Lady's messages to our age through the most recent approved messages of Our Lady of All Nations at Amsterdam and Akita. It was just about to come off the press 7/7/96.

(Three other books I had written in these past few years, after being relieved of the responsibility for the Blue Army, were *Her Glorious Title*, *The Meaning of Akita*, and translation with commentary of Father Yasuda's book *Akita, the Tears and Message*. All three helped in writing *Now the Woman Shall Conquer*.)

The Vigils

These last two books, being rushed for the retreat five days later, were of course very much on my mind on "the" day.

One of the two, *Night of Love*, had been written for those who make all night vigils from the evening of the First Friday to the morning of First Saturday. It had long been out of print and there had been so many requests from vigilers, that for at least fifteen years, I had intended getting out a new edition.

An inspiration to many vigilers is the belief that for *each person* who makes a vigil *a thousand souls, who would otherwise be lost, will be saved.*

The belief was based on a true story told by St. Aphonsus Liguori, a doctor of the Church.

A nun, with whom the Saint was well acquainted, felt inspired one day to make a novena to save a *thousand* souls. But about half way through, she thought that was too much to ask. So, as she was about to say the next novena prayer, she cut the number down. According to Saint Alphonsus, Our

---

[60] The original title of the book was simply *Now* but to make it more specific we added *The Woman Shall Conquer*. It is published by The 101 Foundation, Asbury, NJ, 08802.

For many years, this book had been out of print. A new edition was about to appear during the very week of 7/7/96.

Lady then spoke to her and said: "Already because of this novena a thousand souls *who otherwise would have been lost* have received the grace of final contrition."

In *Night of Love,* I had written: "If a thousand souls could be saved by a novena, how much more should we have this hope for a vigil which responds to the *appeal of the Hearts of Jesus and Mary* on the first Friday and first Saturday...not only for the short time They ask, *but with an entire night!*"

In 1970 I had the privilege of inaugurating a vigil at St. John's Church in New York (next to Madison Square Garden). The Rev. Armand Dasseville, O.F.M.Cap., inspired by the sacrifice and fervor during that first vigil felt impelled to exclaim from the pulpit after the closing Mass:

"I am convinced that *for every person* who made this vigil tonight, *a thousand souls were saved.*"

Praise of Cardinal

Vigils have been continuing at St. John's ever since. In 1995, after 25 successive years, Cardinal O'Connor told the vigilers: "Your prayers are helping not only the city of New York, but *you are helping to save the entire world.*"

Similar vigils are held in towns and cities all around the globe. The book *Night of Love* was used in many of them until copies became tattered and there was repeated demand for a new edition. But I had just never gotten around to doing it, until now...

As I write this I am myself somewhat amazed at all the projects in which I was engaged on that day I did not die.

There was still another in which I was very deeply involved. It was another new foundation just being established in Portugal to provide for the permanent memorial to the Queen of the World mentioned at the end of Chapter Four.

Chapter Twenty-Two

THE FATIMA-OUREANA
FOUNDATION

*Perhaps an entire book would be needed to
cover this subject adequately, but I will try to
summarize why this Castle was chosen as the
ideal place in all the world to honor
Our Lady as its Queen.*

As the reader has already been told more than
once, prior to what seemed a mandate from
Heavenly visitors on 7/7/96, at 81 years of age I had
no intention whatever of writing another book. And
certainly I would not have thought to write about
what I was doing personally in the summer of 1996,
which included a new foundation in Portugal.

As I write this, I realize that if it were not for what
happened on 7/7/96, perhaps I might never have
written an explanation of the monument at the Fatima
Castle described briefly in an earlier chapter, and of
the Foundation to perpetuate it.

The Ideal Place

The Foundation, with extensive property at the
Fatima castle, has provided a museum (perhaps the
only one in the world) dedicated to the Queenship of
Mary.[61] It is near the Castle Cathedral facing a park
maintained by the government of Ourem in honor of

Bishop John Venancio, the Bishop of Fatima who accompanied peace flights of the International Pilgrim Virgin to all the continents of the world and came to be called "The Bishop of the Queen of the World."

Perhaps an entire book would be needed to cover this subject adequately, but I will try to summarize why this Castle was chosen and why it may be considered the ideal place in all the world to honor Our Lady as its Queen.

Significance of the Name

The Castle was named Ourem, in the 12th century, after it was captured from the Moors. Previously the castle had been called simply "the Unconquerable."

Fortified by the Romans, it was the center of government in this central part of Portugal for over two thousand years.

---

[61] At the time of the publication of this book, the museum was temporarily housing historical artifacts. Completion was scheduled for the year 2001, centenary of the first International Marian Congress (held in Fribourg, Switzerland, in 1901), when Pope Leo XIII crowned Our Lady Queen of the World.

During five hundred of those years it was held by Muslims. When they surrendered the castle to the first king of Portugal, a Muslim princess, who took the Christian name, Oureana, married a Portuguese knight. *Before her conversion, the name of the princess was FATIMA.* When she died, she was buried on the opposite hill at a spot which came to bear her Muslim name *Fatima*, while the name of the Castle was changed to her Christian name, Oureana...since reduced to Ourem.

A question I have often asked myself is both why and how this relatively insignificant figure in history, who lived only one year after her conversion to Christianity, could have caused the name of one of the most important castles of Portugal to have been changed (after more than a thousand years) to her Christian name, which it bears to this day, while *the spot where Our Lady was crowned Queen of the World bears her original Muslim name, Fatima*...the same as the name of the daughter of Mohammed. It seems that God arranged this, and for an important reason.

Connection to Our Lady

When his daughter Fatima died, Mohammed said: *"She has the highest place in Heaven after the Virgin Mary."*

Those words are in the Koran, the Mohammedan holy book. They may ultimately be the key to the conversion of Islam which teaches that the dignity of a woman derives from her relationship to a man. So, if Fatima, the daughter of the founder of Islam, has the highest place in Heaven after Our Lady, it follows that Jesus must have the highest place in Heaven.

The Pope chose to name Our Lady of Fatima, Queen of the WORLD, because at Fatima She promised an era of peace *"to all mankind."* And after the conversion of the Communist world, which seems well on its way, the key to that peace is the conversion of the more than one billion Muslims, who today are its major obstacle.

Archbishop Sheen said: "I do not ask why Our Lady appeared in Portugal, the land dedicated to Her. But why did She choose that remote spot named *Fatima*, the only place in all Europe bearing that name?"

Answering his own question the famous Archbishop said he believed it was because Our Lady came not only for the conversion of Russia (which would ultimately mean all the Communist world), *but also for the conversion of Islam.*

So the first reason why it is fitting that the perpetual monument to the Queen of the World should be at the Ourem Castle, through the Fatima-Oureana Foundation, is found in the name itself.

By God's Choice

A second reason is by process of elimination.

We could list many places which might be chosen as the "Marian Capital of the world," as Pope John Paul II referred to Fatima.

Rome would be one of them. But at the very moment the Pope crowned the *Salus Populi Romani* over the tomb of Peter, instituting the Feast of the Queenship of Mary, the Pope recalled that "I first crowned Her Queen of the World at Fatima."

And Pope John Paul II did not refer to Fatima as the "Marian Capital of the World" because Fatima is the greatest Marian Shrine in the world. Several other Shrines, both as regards size and numbers of pilgrims, could claim that title.

It all comes down to a matter of God's Choice. And here the reason of name, and the reason of designation by the Popes, blend into one.

But why should the Castle be the place for the monument rather than the place of the apparitions on the opposite hill? Here again two answers blend.

Historic Place of Authority

The Castle was the center of both civil and religious AUTHORITY in the area of Fatima for the past thousand years. One does not fully understand Fatima without knowing the extraordinary history of this castle.

After being Muslim, Ourem became a court in which most of the languages of Europe were spoken. Its insignia became the Eagle of Savoy, long before nations like Poland and Russia, with that same escutcheon, were kingdoms. On the gate of this castle is still to be seen the coat of arms which links dynasties from the Muslims, to the day a king of Portugal placed his crown before a statue of the Immaculate Conception, proclaiming Her henceforth the Sovereign of the realm.

As we mentioned in describing the unveiling of the Queenship monument at the Castle on Aug. 22, 1996 (only a few weeks after "the" day!), from the site of the monument one can see the stone plaque placed at the gate by command of the king in 1646 proclaiming that Mary Immaculate is its Queen. And from the same site one sees, piercing the sky on the opposite hill, the tower of the Basilica of Fatima...and the Byzantine dome of the International Center of the Blue Army. (Until very recent years these were the two highest points at Fatima.)

It is Fitting

A final reason is that for which philosophers use the Latin word: *Conveniens.*

There are now many monuments at Fatima. There are monuments to the Popes who have prayed there. There are monuments and tombs to Bishops and to the children to whom Our Lady appeared. There is a large remnant of the Berlin wall. More monuments are sure to follow.

Does it not seem fitting that some appropriate but separate place, linked historically to Fatima, should be chosen for a distinctive and *unique* monument to Our Lady of Fatima as the Queen of the World? And the more one knows the history of the Ourem Castle (which is of course also the Castle of Fatima), the more fitting it appears that here there should be the special monument to our universal Queen.

The history is too long to be included here, but at least we can briefly tell the rather amazing story about how the Fatima Castle came to be chosen for Her monument.

How It Came About

In 1945, the last year of the second world war, I published the first English biography of Blessed Nuno, the third Count of Ourem. He had been beatified during the first world war as a model for soldiers. It was primarily because of this book that I came to know the first bishop of Fatima.

His Excellency had always had special devotion to Blessed Nuno. He told me in my first meeting with him that *he had always thought that Our Lady had appeared here at Fatima, in the County of Ourem,* because in Heaven *Blessed Nuno had been asking Her all these years,* that since She was going to come to the world as its Queen to establish a universal era of peace, *that She should choose this place.*

His thought is not to be taken lightly. One prominent writer pointed out that there were not just four persons involved in the apparitions of Fatima (Our Lady and the three children) but five: Our Lady, the three children, and the bishop. The inscription on his tomb in the Basilica of Fatima reads: *Here lies the Bishop of Our Lady.*

Fatima in the Context of History

As the reader knows, I was preoccupied with drawing the attention of the world to the urgency of

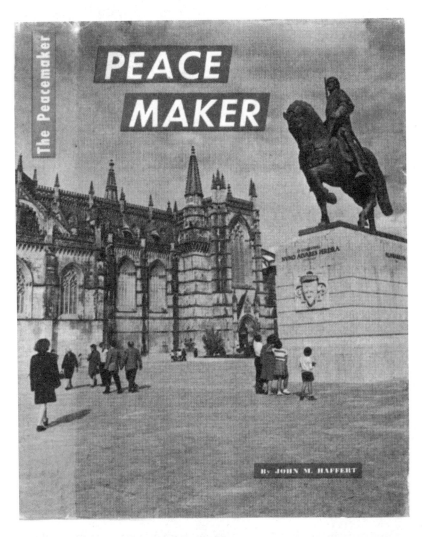

This is the book which started it all: The life of Blessed Nun Alvarez Pereira, the third Count of Ourem and the "George Washington" of Portugal. His monumental statue is seen here beside the great monastery to Our Lady of Victories at the foot of the Fatima mountain.

the message of Fatima ever since I "experienced" it in 1946. And at that time there were no hotels there.

Since getting there and back from Lisbon took up to six hours because of the narrow mountain roads, most people who came to Fatima from all over the world *were there for no more than two or three hours!* And usually most of that time was spent in having lunch.

So I got the idea of serving lunch at the Castle, and during the meal to present the message of Fatima in the context of its history...at the same time getting across the essential message. The program was recorded in English, French, German, Portuguese, Spanish, Italian, and over the years perhaps as many as a hundred thousand pilgrims have seen it.

Here, in a program at the Fatima castle, Queen St. Elizabeth of Portugal is portrayed presenting a rose to Bishop John Venancio. The program shows how the entire history of Portugal leads up to the events of Fatima.

At left is his Royal Highness, the Duke of Braganza and Count of Ourem, at the Castle banquet. Right is John Haffert, on whom the Duke conferred the royal order of the Immaculate Conception (which was inaugurated in 1646, when the royal crown of Portugal was given to Our Lady). They are offering Grace.

To safeguard the integrity of the program, we acquired a considerable amount of property at the Castle, including the most important property to the right and left of the Castle towers. The choicest of these is where the Queenship monument now stands in its primitive form. An entire park will eventually surround it. The present monument itself will be enriched as funds permit.

At the top of the castle, the government has created a park with magnificent panoramic views in all directions, at the center of which is a monumental statue of Blessed Nuno.

One might dare to say that this is one of the most beautiful historic squares in all the world.

An area where there had previously been a medieval house is now the park dedicated to Bishop Venancio, "Bishop of the Queen of the World." Three ancient houses adjoining it are now a museum which will contain relics, artifacts, and depictions of all the major apparitions of Our Lady as Queen, from the Rue du Bac to Fatima...please God, until Her victory is complete and the era of peace for MANKIND is here.

We are privileged to have as one of the trustees of the foundation a direct descendant of Blessed Nuno, his Royal Highness Don Duarte Pio de Braganza (His godfather was Pope Pius XII, after whom he was named). If the monarchy is restored, he will be king of Portugal and, indeed, most Portuguese refer to him as their king. His predecessor on the throne of Portugal died in exile in England. During the years of exile, he signed all his documents and letters simply as "The Count of Ourem."

His Highness is not a trustee just in name. He is vitally interested, attends all the meetings, and because of his wide learning and refinement, is of inestimable value to the foundation.

Almost equally important is the Rev. Father Carlos, Prior of Ourem, who is in charge not only of the Cathedral within the Castle walls, but has six other parishes immediately dependent upon him in the area between the Castle and the Shrine of Fatima. He is one of the signatories of the Foundation and is in daily contact with the Director, Mr. Carlos Evaristo, a former journalist, with special interest in relics and archaeology, who seems uniquely qualified to manage the museum and the castle program.

The program and the museum present the message of Fatima in the context of history. In that context, we can see the Providence of God over the centuries leading to this present moment, when the Pope said:

"As we approach the millennium, it seems that the words of Our Lady of Fatima are nearing their fulfillment."

Perhaps, like myself, the reader was puzzled by that strange expression on which Our Lady *insisted* in Her appearances in Amsterdam: "Our Lady of All Nations, *who once was Mary.*"

We deserve chastisement, but God enables Our Lady to appear now at Fatima in triumphant power, confirmed by "the greatest and most colossal miracle in history."

At Fatima, Our Lady wore only two adornments, two signs:

1) The globe worn about Her neck which symbolized "the world and each individual person;"

2) A Star at the hem of Her robe which, according to Abbe André Richard, author of several books on Fatima, refers to the prefigurement of Our Lady in the Old Testament figure of Queen Esther (which means star).

"To understand Fatima," the famous French author said, "read the book of Esther." It is the account of a *queen who saved her people from annihilation* by her intercession before the king.

Lady of All Nations

It is to emphasize today's role of Our Lady as a powerful and conquering Queen...Woman of the Apocalypse...that God wishes to emphasize Her role NOW by telling us to pray to *The Lady of All Nations* who *once*, that is *in the past*, was simply known as Mary...Mary the Maid of Nazareth, Mary hidden in Scripture, Mary at the foot of the Cross, powerless to save Her Son, but *now empowered to conquer*.

I have already written of this in *NOW*, one of the two books just coming off the press on "the" day which I have already mentioned. But it is so relevant to all we hope to accomplish through LAF, and also through the Fatima-Oureana Foundation, that I repeat it here.

We tend to be fascinated by Her words concerning future events, especially of possible chastisement. *But there are more important words and events upon which we must meditate,* in the context of two thousand years of Christian History.

It is the purpose of the monument and museum at the castle of Ourem not only to honor Our Lady as Queen of the World, but to help the world respond to Her request: *"Remember my words."* We are too often anxious to hear new words and overlook the lessons of history engraved, as it were, for all to see in this monument and museum. Her message has not changed since the apparitions to St. Catherine Labouré almost two hundred years ago. It has only become more urgent.

The author is shown standing behind his Carmelite sister, on one of the very rare occasions she was permitted to make a family visit. To her right and left are her father and mother. A more remarkable family visit took place on June 10, 1998, on the occasion of the 60th wedding anniversary of her brother, Horace (standing, right). She had been expected to die less than two years before, and to be physically incapacitated if she did survive.

Chapter Twenty-Three

URGENCY OF THE MESSAGE

What was on my mind in the summer of 1996 was exactly the same as on the day I first knelt in the Chapel of the Apparitions at Fatima, just fifty years before, and realized that Our Lady had come to prevent the annihilation of entire nations. She had come to remind us of the basic truths of our faith, and to make it possible for mankind to avert a chastisement worse than the deluge.

I have written at length in almost all my books, and especially in *To Prevent This!*, that the mission of the Blue Army is urgent, because it is urgent to save souls, and because the threat of atomic destruction will be with us as long as there is a single bomb on the earth.

As we said before, somewhat at length, the *Fatima pledge* (extending the morning offering throughout the day, with the help of the Rosary and Scapular and First Saturday devotions) *is a like a magic formula of holiness*. **This formula is the great gift of Our Lady to our time.** *Through the Blue Army, it has set hundreds of thousands on the path of holiness.* This mission will not be over until every person in the world is a saint.[62] In the meantime, it could prevent, or at least mitigate, the purging of the world by fire.

No More Battle Cry

One reason the Blue Army declined so precipitously in such a few years, as I said in Chapter 13, is that under the new direction, the sense of urgency was being lost. The Blue Army had rallied millions with the battle cry *"Russia will be converted."* Now, with the Soviet Union dissolved and victory almost in sight, the Battle Cry *"To prevent the chastisement!"* was forbidden.

Perhaps my greatest disappointment was the decision of the Blue Army's new directors not to release our major motion picture film *State of Emergency*, which was based on the words of Our Lady: "Several entire nations will be annihilated."

State of Emergency Canceled

The film had been produced with Hollywood professionals to "shake the world" into awareness of the impending chastisement if men continued to ignore that bottom line of the Fatima message: *"Men must cease offending God, Who is already so much offended."*

I took the responsibility of this film very, very seriously. I felt it could not be accomplished without much prayer. Through *SOUL*'s large circulation, we obtained pledges from *thousands* to say a special prayer *every day* for this intention. Many said the prayer daily for several years. Thousands gladly *sacrificed five million dollars to produce it.* (It would probably cost twice as much today).

I selected a director who was a practicing Catholic, and a writer who believed in the Fatima message. The film, *based on the true life story of a scientist who worked on the first atomic bomb and felt hopeless about the future*

---

62 To understand the importance of this formula, and the devotion of the first Saturdays, we urgently recommend the book *To Prevent This!*, published by The 101 Foundation, Asbury, NJ, 08802.

of the world until he learned of Fatima, was produced in France and Portugal starring Martin Sheen. It was approved by Bishop Hastrich and the national committee. The preview in Hollywood gave it a very high (83%) approval rating. I had sent videotapes of the film to many of the major donors. One of them

This is one of the original posters of the film STATE OF EMERGENCY, based on the true life experience of an atomic scientist who found hope in the message of Fatima.

wrote to say he had viewed it *forty-three times,* adding: "Each time I seem to find something new. It is a GREAT film."

Recently My Hopes Had Been Raised

After my many objections, only ten months before 7/7/96, I received a letter from the new Blue Army director saying that the board had decided the film was mine to do with as I wished.

Within a week, I had a commitment of funds for the update of the film and its immediate release. The director of the film, Richard Bennett, had agreed that Martin Sheen would again star, this time as the atomic scientist in old age reminiscing about his experience depicted in the film.

Then, just as we were about to go ahead, *another letter came to stop it.* It said, without any explanation, the Blue Army had now decided to *destroy* the film.

I always believed this film to be one of the most important projects of our Fatima apostolate. I still have that faith. I threatened court action on behalf of the thousands who had donated to make the film, if it were destroyed.

Now that we know the message of Akita, which is the third secret of Fatima, *State of Emergency* could be more powerful today than when it was made. On March 25, 1998, the current direction of the Blue Army gave assurance that the film was safely in storage.

New Direction Refuses Akita

One of the last issues of *SOUL* which I edited (at the end of 1984) told the message of Akita. Fortunately, on the basis of the accepted average of four to five per copy, the magazine was then reaching a million readers.

But the new direction seemed to have decided against any mention of *chastisement. Mention of Akita was forbidden!* A major motion picture telling all the world that there could be a chastisement "worse than the deluge" had to be destroyed.

The reader may begin to understand the bewilderment I was feeling on 7/7/96, when it seemed that Bishop Venancio and Bishop Hastrich were telling me to write about what I was doing and why, therefore, to write of this so extensively in Chapter 13.

Our Lady had appeared at Akita on the actual anniversary of the Fatima miracle in 1973 to tell us that time was running out. She said, with miracles of tears, if the world did not stop sinning, and if reparation was not made, there would be a chastisement worse than the deluge. And it was precisely when Pope John Paul II made the collegial consecration to the Immaculate Heart of Mary in 1984 that the pastoral letter was issued approving the message of Akita.

Our Lady was updating Her Fatima message, making known the third secret (as confirmed by Cardinal Ratzinger), and Her own apostolate was ignoring it.

But Things WERE Happening!

But, God raised up many other voices to echo the cry over the world. Dr. Turton formed the 101 Foundation specifically to make Akita known. Her Foundation published books the Blue Army now refused.

There were weeping statues and frequently reported apparitions of Our Lady. The Marian Movement of Priests began to cover the world, stressing the urgency of our response. Marian Conferences were held. Apostolates from Centers of Peace rose up in almost every nation. One single individual in the U.S., Dr. Thomas Petrisko, distributed the messages, in newspaper format, millions of copies at a time.

Spreading from the Philippines throughout the entire world, *the Fatima pledge was being promoted by*

A STATE OF EMERGENCY!

This is one of the posters proposed for an update of the film in which Martin Sheen plays the part of the scientist he portrayed in the original film, but now as an older man, remembering. Beyond the mushroom cloud is the "hidden" image of Our Lady who said at Akita that the world would experience a chastisement, "worse that the deluge," if Her message is not heard.

the Alliance, together with the message of enthronement of the Sacred Hearts in homes and Communions
of reparation. As mentioned above, its spread seemed
almost miraculous (especially in the Third World),
emphasizing the first Saturday devotion, with an
urgent invitation to make the first Friday–first
Saturday vigil.

Incidentally, this almost miraculous spread of
consecration to the Sacred Hearts (implemented by
the pledge and the first Friday-first Saturday
devotions) had been prophesied. While sponsored by
a group of six bishops, headed by Cardinal Vidal, *it
was guided every step of the way by the Sacred Heart*
through a hidden messenger, a seminarian.

New Phenomenon: Traveling Messengers

And this has been a new phenomenon: persons
(usually laity) receiving messages from Heaven and
often commanded to go forth, even to foreign lands.
The messages are *almost invariably the same as the
message of Fatima,* with slight variations. All say that
response is urgent.

Jesus had said that, if necessary, the very stones
would cry out.

And, if God would cause wooden and plaster
statues to weep in order to get our attention, would
He not cause devout persons to speak?

Most of these messages, as I said above, are mere
affirmations of what Our Lady has said in approved
apparitions which often, as in the case of Akita,
have not been sufficiently heeded. Specifically to a
visionary supported by her bishop, Our Lady said the
world would be saved if enough persons lived the
morning offering with aid of the Scapular and Rosary.
Almost all messages stress the Rosary.

Paula Albertini, for example, knew no English
when Our Lady told her to go to the United States,
and then told her to go to see Mother Angelica. When
Paula asked Mother Angelica to pray the Rosary with

her, in humility and faith, the founder of EWTN did so. After the third decade, Mother Angelica laid aside the braces she had worn for forty years. Viewers of the Eternal Word Television Network were stunned. Mother Angelica had long talked about *the power of the Rosary.* Now millions *witnessed it.*

Paula Albertini had been at Marian Manor in Asbury, NJ, at the invitation of Dr. Turton, within a few days before she went to Alabama to see Mother Angelica.

What if Mother Angelica had said "I don't believe in such things," or "I haven't time for people like that," or "We don't need to give attention to lay people who say they have messages from Heaven," or "We have to wait until the Church tells us who is authentic," or any of the many similar reasons good people have for denying that today God raises up prophets in our midst.

But Mother Angelica saw that Paula was a simple, humble person, as are all authentic messengers.

We have difficulty accepting messengers of God perhaps because they are usually quite ordinary people. Do we ever stop to consider what it costs them to say "Jesus told me," or "Our Lady told me," to a sceptical world? I had a glimpse of what it cost when I interviewed Sister Lucia, the visionary of Fatima, in 1946, almost 50 years to the day of 7/7/96.

The Armchair

While waiting for her in the parlor, I had moved an armchair to the edge of a divan expecting that Sister would sit in the chair and I would then be very close to her on the end of the divan where I had placed my briefcase,

Sister Lucia immediately went and removed the heavy armchair.

With dismay, I thought she had decided to move farther from where I would be sitting. But next she placed a plain chair in its place. She had moved the more comfortable chair to be used by the Prioress. She herself sat where I had hoped...but in a simple, straight chair.

Three things struck me: 1) The simplicity with which this was done; 2) The kindness; 3) The ease with which she had moved that chair, which I had discovered to be quite heavy! Obviously, this was a person very much in command of herself, naturally humble (what she did seemed almost instinctive), and thoughtful.

Off Guard

I had previously known a saintly person (the first steps of his cause of beatification having already begun), and I knew that the more one advances in the Light of God the more one is aware of personal faults and imperfections. I could see that Sister Lucia did not look on herself as a "special" person in any way. She simply felt that Our Lady had to choose someone for Her great message to the world and she happened to be the one...not because she was worthy, but simply as a matter of God's choice.

This is characteristic of any authentic prophet. (I use the word "prophet" in its true meaning: A messenger.)

I had not come to see a saint or a visionary. *I had come to talk to a messenger of Our Lady.* And my only interest, quite truly, was to understand the message. Sister Lucia grasped this, and we were speaking together so naturally that now something happened unexpectedly, which gave me a glimpse into her heart.

I asked her about recent apparitions of Our Lady of which the Bishop of Fatima had spoken to me. She said she could not speak of them. "But, Sister," I said, "the Bishop told me..." and I went on to speak of two recent visits of Our Lady. She seemed very surprised that the Bishop had spoken to me of them. And I asked: "And when Our Lady appears to you, Sister, is it always the same?"

HER OWN WORDS to the Nuclear Age

This cover of one of Haffert's most important books suggests the concerns of Lucia, left in the world as the messenger of its Queen.

In that moment, since we had been conversing so naturally, she forgot herself and gazed upward with what to me was an indescribable look, as she almost whispered: "Yes, the same...always the same."

There was such a wistfulness in her voice that I realized that *here was a soul in exile*. When Our Lady had announced that She would come "soon" for Francis and Jacinta, but that Lucia would have to remain on earth, she said it was as though a sword had pierced her heart. She had a glimpse of Heaven. Earth had become purgatory.

The Offense

Earth is probably Purgatory for all who are given messages from Heaven. They are almost invariably maligned, often in high places.[63] They truly suffer when told to speak.

A priest who was with me during this interview with Sr. Lucia reached out to touch his Rosary to her hand. She instinctively withdrew as though she had been struck.

I had the same reaction once when someone called me a saint. I knew just how she felt.

She felt that Our Lady chose her because she is a nobody...a once illiterate, simple mountain child. She felt a nostalgia for family, for Francis, for Jacinta. She felt an exile on this earth. And she felt a terrible responsibility because she knew better than anyone else on earth how important it was for the world to respond to the messages entrusted to her.

---

[63] It seems that the more these messengers become known, the more they are persecuted. Some are judged without trial and burned at the stake of public condemnation without the evidence of their spiritual directors ever being heard.

This is a rarely seen picture of the three children of Fatima. Lucia is in the middle. She said it was as though a sword pierced her heart when Our Lady said She would come soon for Francis and Jacinta, but that Lucia had to remain as Her messenger.

Why Messengers in Our Midst?

We may ask: Why are there so many messengers today, and why did God keep Sister Lucia in exile here so many years?

In 1998, a new tomb was waiting for her in the Basilica of Fatima, next to Jacinta, across the nave from Francis. But Heaven had not needed her as we did.

How reassuring it has been to persons like myself to know that she was still here to answer questions...as those about the Scapular to Fr. Howard Rafferty, about the first Saturdays, about the collegial consecration, and on and on! Her presence in this world was a constant evidence of the timeliness and urgency of the Fatima Message which, in his letter of Oct. 13, 1997, Pope John Paul II called one of the *greatest signs of the times,* and he had previously said:

"As we approach the millennium, it seems that the words of Our Lady of Fatima are nearing their fulfillment."

The fact that God left Sister Lucia in our midst for so many years sustained us in that hope. And if these few words can help to convey even a vague idea of how she *actually felt* as she continued here in exile, may we understand others who are messengers of God when they are sent to us.[64] Let us pray for them as they suffer and pray for us. And if a message *is*

The little girl is standing on the spot in the Basilica of Fatima, next to the tomb of Jacinta, where a tomb now awaits Lucia.

---

[64] Those entrusted with messages from Heaven are fallible men and women and their mission does not suddenly make them saints. Perhaps it is best not to seek them out, while at the same time remaining open if they come to us. The first question to ask is whether they come with the support of their bishop or of a reliable priest-director. We are obliged to reject any message not consonant with the teaching of the Church.

confirmed by miracles and approved by the Church, as in the case of Fatima and Akita, *let us respond without doubt or hesitation.*

We are in critical times and God does not deprive us of His Voice. We are deprived if we do not listen.

*The main source book on Akita, **Akita, the Tears and Message of Mary**, was translated by John Haffert into English, at the request of the Bishop of Akita, the Most Rev. John S. Ito. That message revealed the third secret of Fatima. Subsequently, in 1989, Mr. Haffert wrote the above book, which the bishop, who knew English, not only approved, but warmly recommended. Within three years, three reprintings followed.*

Chapter Twenty-Four

THE CHASTISEMENT CAN BE AVERTED

*When prophesying that various nations
will be annihilated, Our Lady said at Fatima:
"To prevent this I shall come to ask for the
consecration of Russia to my Immaculate Heart
and Communions of Reparation on first
Saturdays." Would She have said, "to prevent
this" if She had not come to prevent it?*

We had been hearing much about a purifying chastisement of the world. Our Lady had said at Akita it would be a fire which would destroy a great part of mankind, a chastisement "worse than the deluge."

Many of the best known and most successful lay apostles of our country gathered for that first retreat, July 11 to July 16, 1996. And one of the questions we addressed was: Can the chastisement be averted?

In the beginning, the majority seemed to think we had to have the purification. But, as the days went on and as we listened to each other, we began to marvel at all that was being done right now to respond to the conditions of Our Lady for Her triumph.

All we saw on television or read in the press was bad news. But good things were happening! The modern messages of Our Lady were not falling on deaf ears. Even if many of our pulpits were silent, hundreds of devout laity were getting out the message.

Then, Bob Ziener, founder of *Rosaries for Peace*, said: "According to St. Thomas, God often threatens chastisements so that we will avoid them."

Another said: "I never thought Our Lady came to promise Her triumph over a world of burned out corpses."

Maureen Flynn, editor and publisher of the slick magazine *Signs and Wonders*, said:

"We would have such power if Marian apostolates would work together. I believe that Our Lady is giving us *not only a call to unity, but also the grace to achieve it.*"

Dr. Tom Petrisko, author of several books and producer of newspaper type publications on Our Lady's messages (five million copies of his latest edition), said:

Dr. Tom Petrisko speaking at the Lay Saints Retreat sponsored by the Lay Apostolate Foundation.

"Our Lady shows us the way. She is an anxious Mother. She tells us, while our sins call for chastisement, She can prevent it if we respond." Then referring to many recent messages alleged to be from Heaven, he added:

"Fatima is the wall on which we see many 'posters' appearing in affirmation of Her urgent call. Everything was said at Fatima. Everything since then is emphasis. And that emphasis, given in many places around the world, often in a miracle of blood and tears, is touching more and more persons with a sense of urgency." There was unanimous agreement.

It would not be fair to single out any one leader, but all would have agreed that the "star" of the five days was Bud MacFarland, Sr. Somehow, in one single talk, he expressed what *everyone* wanted to say: The signs of the times (of which Pope John Paul said in his Oct. 13, 1997 letter), Fatima is one of the greatest cry out to us. It is urgent that we respond by prayer, fasting, action. He said: "Fasting is so important! We should strive to fast on bread and water on Mondays, Wednesdays, and Fridays. God hears especially the prayers of those sincere enough to fast."

Anatol Kaszczuk, who founded both the Legion of Mary and the Blue Army in Poland, and also initiated Rosary congresses all over the world, stressed the importance of the first Saturday devotion and of the first Friday to first Saturday vigils. He said that these vigils, which are being made by more and more generous souls, could weigh in the balance of Divine Justice.

Alfred Williams, who, as custodian of the national U.S. Pilgrim Virgin, had spoken to hundreds of thousands throughout America about the message of Fatima, recalled:

"When prophesying that various nations will be annihilated, Our Lady said at Fatima: 'To prevent this I shall come to ask for the consecration of Russia to my Immaculate Heart and Communions of Reparation on first Saturdays.' Would She have said 'to prevent this' if She had not come to prevent it?"

Tremendous Experience

We now hold these five day retreats every year on the same dates: July 11–16 (including the anniversary of the July Fatima apparition and the Feast of the Scapular). Since they are on the same dates, one can plan long ahead to attend. Similar retreats, using professional videos we have made of all our speakers, may be held *anywhere*, with virtually no expense, even by a few.

Thomas M. Fahy, who for 23 years had been promoting the cause and the works of the Ven. Luisa Picaretta (official U.S. postulator of her cause), said about this Lay Saints Retreat:

"This was the most pleasant experience of its kind since my childhood innocence. It was a peek into the future of how things will be after the great triumph of the Immaculate Heart of Mary."

We were especially blessed in this retreat with several exceptional priests including Father Redemptus Valabek, O.Carm., from Rome, who deals on an international level with the lay apostolate (I mentioned him before as my host in Rome in June).

Perhaps the reason it was such a wonderful experience for all these zealous apostles (we were about fifty in all) was the community of spirit. So many lay persons work alone, sometimes without adequate ecclesiastical support. They found joy and inspiration in each other.

Urgent Challenge

We were dismayed to learn that while we were only beginning to organize, a group calling itself *We Are the Church* was obtaining signatures to a petition for married priests, for contraception, etc. It was reported in the press that they had *seven million* petitions signed while, behind the scenes, *an effort was being made to remove Pope John Paul II.*

The lead article of the subsequent Nov. 1996 issue of the magazine *Inside the Vatican* said those opposing the Pope were considering a new ruling to limit the term of the papacy (which is now for life), or to make retirement mandatory at age 80, since all Cardinals after 80 cannot vote in a papal election. *Inside the Vatican* said this was not just an effort to change this Pope, but to change the very nature of the papacy.

We saw the great need for an immediate response by the devout Catholic laity, who for so many years have been inactive. We felt certain they would surely rise, at least with sacrifice and prayer, in the face of a threat to the papacy itself.

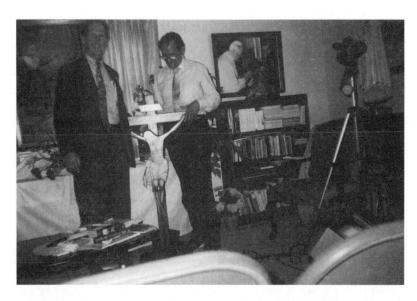

Bud MacFarland with the author at the Lay Saints Retreat.

Chapter Twenty-Five

"POOR HOLY FATHER!"

When Our Lord showed Blessed Elizabeth Mora that Pius VII was surrounded by counselors with the aspect of wolves, Elizabeth saved the Pope. In the vision of Jacinta, we saw our present Pope endangered. Would we save him?

S hortly after the apparitions of Our Lady at Fatima, in which Our Lady pleaded for reparation, Jacinta saw a vision reported by Lucia in her memoirs: *"I saw the Holy Father in a very big house kneeling by a table with his head buried in his hands, and he was weeping. Outside the house there were many people. Some of them were throwing stones, others were cursing him and using bad language. Poor Holy Father! We must pray very hard for him!"*

"Is the one I saw weeping...the one Our Lady told us about in the secret?" she asked Lucia. Lucia replied that it was.

"Can't I say that I saw the Holy Father and all those people?" Jacinta asked,

"No," Lucia replied, *"don't you see that is **part of the secret**?"*

Only now the famous secret has been made known. In the message given at Akita, which was confirmed by Cardinal Ratzinger as the same as the third secret of Fatima,[65] Our Lady said: *"The work of the devil*

*Pope John Paul II carries the Eucharist at Fatima which
he called "The Marian Capital of the World." Although any
of the Popes since 1917 could have been the Pope of
Jacinta's vision, it seems most probable that it is John Paul
II. We see a connection with the last secret of Fatima not
revealed until March of 1984, when this Pope, victim a
few years earlier of attempted assassination, made the
collegial consecration to the Immaculate Heart. It was
because of the secret, that Jacinta could not make public her
vision of the suffering Pope in 1917.*

---

[65] The message of Akita was approved in 1984. On
three separate occasions, Cardinal Ratzinger, custodian
of the Fatima secret, said the message of Akita was the
same. Cf: **Now the Woman Shall Conquer**, by J. M.
Haffert, published in 1997 by The 101 Foundation,
Asbury, NJ.

will infiltrate even into the Church in such a way that one will see cardinals opposing cardinals, bishops against other bishops...the Church will be full of those who accept compromises..."[66]

Urgency

The words of little Jacinta seemed to cry out to us: "Poor Holy Father! WE MUST PRAY **VERY HARD** FOR HIM!"

A sign of hope was the very fact that this effort against the Pope, which had been gathering strength for at least four years,[67] is no longer secret. Word was spreading in a marvelous way throughout the entire world. Already many thousands of messages and prayers supporting the Holy Father were being sent to him.

After the retreat, the Foundation took care to verify the reports and then prepared a bulletin which was sent to its 1,200 advisors (most of whom are daily communicants) for criticism. Then 50,000 copies were mailed, and it spread to other countries

Would there be enough ordinary Catholics responding? Could their prayers and support enable the Holy Father to fulfill the special mission described in his

---

[66] *The Meaning of Akita* by John M. Haffert, published by The 101 Foundation, p. 4. Note: This book was read and endorsed by the Most Rev. John Ito, the Bishop of Akita who approved the Akita apparitions in 1984.

[67] We read in *Dictionary of the Life and Teachings of John Paul II,* published 1994: "Do things appear to expose the faithful to such a happening now?... The possibility depends on the number opposed to him (John Paul II), their readiness to take extreme measures, their calculation of the ultimate support that will be forthcoming. They might be ruthless, motivated by a perverse desire to change the direction of the Church" (p. 4, under *Anti-Pope*).

apostolic letter: *to lead the Church into the millennium "in the hope of the definitive coming of the Kingdom?"*

It is of special interest that God used lay persons in the past to save the Papacy.

How did Catherine, a Lay Woman, do it?

More than thirty times in the past, Cardinals have elected a new Pope while the rightful Pope was still living and competent. In 1330, after only two years, the antipope of that time submitted in Avignon to Pope John XXII in one of the darkest times when the papacy had been moved to Avignon from Rome. *Finally it was a laywoman, member of the third Order of St. Dominic, who succeeded in bringing the Popes from Avignon back to Rome. She was St. Catherine of Siena.*[68]

How did she do it? How even did she get to see the pope, let alone persuade him to return to Rome and put an end to these dark times? *She organized a campaign of prayer.*

How did St. Nicholas, a Layman, Respond?

The last time Cardinals declared a Pope "removed" and elected an Anti-Pope was in the time of St. Nicholas of Flue, a family man with ten children.

Our Lord revealed to Nicholas the long-lasting, devastating effects this would have. Soon afterwards came the revolt of Martin Luther, resulting in more than 200 DIFFERENT Christian churches! *Our Lord told him:*

"O my children, do not let yourselves be misled by any innovations! Stay together and hold fast. Stay on the same way, the same paths as your pious ancestors. That is how you will resist the attacks, tempests, and storms that are going to rise up with violence."[69]

---

[68] St. Catherine was a Dominican in the world, a member of the third Order.

[69] *Saint Nicholas*, by Pere Clement, p. 53.

In reparation, St. Nicholas arranged his family affairs, and with permission of his wife, lived as a hermit. During the last twenty years of his life, he lived only on the Holy Eucharist. He was given a vision of *the apostasy of the latter times.* Prophesying perhaps what we are experiencing now, he wrote:

"The Church will be punished because the majority of its members, great and small, will become very perverted. (We are told that today as many as 80% of Catholics in some countries do not follow the Pope's teachings on chastity according to one's state of life.) *The Church will sink deeper and deeper until it finally seems to have been destroyed and the succession of Peter and the other Apostles will seem to have ended."* Could even a remnant of faithful Catholics *now* save the Pope?

Bl. Elizabeth Mora Did It!

The last greatest crisis in the Church was when Pius VI was taken from Rome and died two years later in exile. His successor, Pius VII, was also arrested and made a prisoner in France.

In this crisis, Our Lord appeared to a Roman housewife who was bearing the difficult cross of abandonment by her husband and struggling in poverty to raise two children. He said:

"My dear daughter, offer yourself to My Heavenly Father for the Church. I promise to help you."

Jesus then showed her a castle which seemed about to fall because of attacks from without and machinations from within. *She saw the Pope assisted by two angels, but surrounded by counselors who had the aspect of wolves.*[70]

Her Response

Blessed Elizabeth did more than offer herself. She did more than just accept the great trials of her life

---

[70] This quote and those following are from her biography by Paola Giovettia, published in Rome in 1992 on the occasion of her beatification.

with loving resignation. *She started a prayer crusade by simply asking all she knew to pray for the Holy Father and for the Church.*

To her consolation and joy, she found another Roman housewife (with seven children), *who had received a similar message from Our Lord to "save the Church."* It was Blessed Anne Marie Taigi who, at the age of nine, *offered her life for the Pope, when told he was in danger.* Elizabeth and Anne Marie became close friends, and by their own prayers and those of others, *they did indeed save the Pope and the Church at that moment.*

How The Pope Was Saved

Pius VII returned to Rome, as everyone knows. But Satan had not finished his efforts to get rid of this Pope. His Holiness was still *surrounded by those counselors with the aspect of wolves.* These highly placed ecclesiastics persuaded him to leave Rome again. *Our Lord revealed to Elizabeth and Anne Marie that a carriage was waiting to take the Pope to a French ship at the nearby port of Civitavecchia.*

Poor Housewives! What Could They Do?

Elizabeth tells us in her diary that immediately *"God deigned to hear my prayer and gave so much agility to my spirit that I was able in a moment to penetrate the papal palace and freely speak...manifesting to the Holy Father the reasons dictated by the Spirit, why he should remain in Rome. His Holiness, despite all counsel and persuasion to the contrary, even though the carriage was waiting to take him away, left all his counselors and said that instead of leaving he wished to remain. This sudden and unexpected decision at once spoiled all the plans made by the malignant ones."*

Elizabeth, whose remarkable life had been hidden, became known when the present Pope beatified her in 1992. It seems that God willed now, after over a hundred years, that the entire Church should know.

There followed a stabilization of the Church. The first Vatican Council defined papal infallibility and shortly afterwards Pope Pius IX defined the dogma of the Immaculate Conception. There followed a sequence of great Popes and an ever increasing stability of the Apostolic Church despite (and perhaps even aided by) the dissolution of the papal states. But, even with the greatest of Popes, we cannot have a triumph of the Church without holiness.

Are There Lay Saints Today?

Are there now faithful lay Catholics like Saint Nicholas, St. Catherine, St. Elizabeth, and Bl. Anne Marie? Is there a sufficient number to respond to a message given by Our Lord in 1944:

"Obey My Pope no matter what comes up. Remain faithful to him and I will give you the graces and the strength you will need. (Almost the very words He spoke to Bl. Elizabeth!) *I urge you to keep faithful to him and keep away from anyone who rebels against him. Above all, never listen to anyone who dispels him..."*[71]

There will always be the faithful who love the Church, like St. Theresa of Avila, who encyclopedist Rev. Michael O'Carroll, D.D., called "the greatest woman in history outside of the Bible." When dying, she said simply, "I am a daughter of the Church!"

"Mobilize the Laity!"

While it is reported that millions of petitions were presented in Rome against the Pope, *several million very different petitions were sent to ask the Holy Father to proclaim as a dogma, that Our Lady is Co-Redemptrix, Mediatrix, and Advocate. And Our Lady Herself has said that the triumph of the Church will then take place.* Are we nearing the climax of a spiritual BATTLE?

Recall that *Our Lord showed Blessed Elizabeth two angels protecting Pius VII, but that he was surrounded by*

---

[71] *Dictionary* (mentioned above), p. 94.

counselors with the aspect of wolves. She did something about it. Can we?

St. Catherine of Siena did. So did Nicholas of Flue. Elizabeth Mora and Anne Marie Taigi teamed together. And was it not to show that the saving of Rome and the stabilization of the papacy was due to THEIR sacrifices and prayers that God sent Elizabeth to the Pope in bilocation *rather than persuading the Pope by His Own Voice?* Was He not showing His Holy Will that we, faithful laity, are to save the Church by our prayers and sacrifices?

These lay persons were asked directly by Our Lord to offer themselves to save the Pope, to save the Church. They responded!

Now Jesus and His mother are calling to each one of us! Appearing as Our Lady of All Nations (apparitions approved May 31, 1996), Our Lady said what She repeated at Akita: *"Cardinals would be against Cardinals, and Bishops against Bishops."* Then, She said: *"The clergy are too few. MOBILIZE THE LAITY!"* [72]

Now A Reality

Now as the vision of Jacinta becomes reality, let us hear that little saint's plea: *"Oh, the poor Holy Father! We must pray very hard for him!"*

On Oct. 11, 1992, in an interview with a faithful Cardinal, Lucia said: *"He that is not with the Pope is not with God, and he that wants to be with God must be with the Pope."*[73]

Pope Paul VI, on the Feast of Sts. Peter and Paul in 1971, said: "He who believes in the Church believes in the Pope. He who believes in the Pope believes in the Church." This is a truth based on the words of Our Lord (Matthew 16:18): "You are Peter (Rock) and on this Rock, I shall build My Church."

---

[72] For full message see *Now The Woman Shall Conquer*, mentioned above.

[73] *Two Hours With Sr. Lucia* by Carlos Evaristo, available from LAF.

Chapter Twenty-Six

DO YOU LOVE ME?

At Fatima, the angel said: "Make of everything you do a sacrifice."

I said in the beginning that one reason I was reluctant to begin this book is because we seem to be drowning in a plethora of new books with no more time for the timeless ones.

Recently, I opened one of those timeless books[74] at random and read again what I had read several times before, but without ever really understanding.

It was the account of the final apparition of "Our Lady of the Golden Heart" which took place in the small town of Beauraing, Belgium, in 1932 and 1933.

In thirty-three apparitions to five children, Our Lady at Beauraing spoke seven times with only short phrases, until the very last apparition. Her words were: "Always be good; I am the Immaculate Virgin; Soon I shall appear for the last time; Pray, pray very much. Pray always; I am the Mother of God, the Queen of Heaven. Pray always; I will convert sinners. Good-bye."

None of those words, even read over and over, seemed to warrant thirty-three apparitions. But something unusual followed her "Good-bye."

---

[74] *The Woman Shall Conquer* by Don Sharkey. Available from The 101 Foundation, Asbury, NJ.

One of the children could not accept that Our Lady was leaving because in that final visit she had not seen Her, so she pleaded with Our Lady and suddenly there was a great flash. There was a ball of fire very much as at Fatima. Then, Our Lady appeared in the hawthorn bush in greater splendor than ever, with almost blinding light shining from Her Heart which appeared to be of gold. She said:

"Do you love my Son?"

"Yes."

"Do you love me?"

"Yes.

"Sacrifice yourself for me."

Then, Her golden heart shone forth in dazzling splendor as she said a final "Good-bye."

I had not only read this in Sharkey's book two or three times (perhaps even more because it is a book I pick up over and over), but I had been several times to the Shrine in Beauraing. On one occasion, I even spent several days there. I had seen those very words inscribed in large letters on the Shrine wall.

Deeper Understanding

But suddenly, *reading it still once again*, it came to have a deeper meaning than ever before. It was "accumulated" understanding perhaps more than some sudden light. And that may be enough reason in itself to read over again, from time to time, certain books whose inexhaustible treasure is in words from Heaven. As our knowledge grows, so does our ability to understand.

I had only recently learned that hawthorn, which has long and sharp thorns, means "holy thorn." The history of the old Marian Shrine in England at Glastonbury is linked to the tradition that Joseph of Arimathea brought a hawthorn there from the Holy Land, the thorn bush from which the crown of thorns of Our Lord had been fashioned.

How much more the apparition of Our Lady *in* the hawthorn bush at Beauraing seemed to mean in that light. At Fatima, She wore the thorns around Her Heart, which represents Her whole person.

Also, I had been puzzled that She came to be known as "Our Lady of the Golden Heart" rather than of the Immaculate Heart. This had always slightly bothered me because gold, however beautiful, seems cold.

But, subsequently, I read in Maria Valtorta's description of the presentation of Our Lord in the Temple, that the holy woman Anne consoled Our Lady (after Simeon had told Her that Her Heart would be pierced by a sword):

"Our God will give you a Heart of most pure gold to withstand the storm of sorrow, so that you will be the greatest woman in creation: *the Mother.*"[75]

Now I delight in thinking of the most pure heart of Mary also as a golden heart, purified by fires which would have destroyed any ordinary heart, meriting the words of Jesus from the cross: *Mother!*

But what struck me more than it had in any previous reading, were those simple words: "Do you love My Son? Do you love me? Sacrifice yourself for me."

At Fatima, the angel said; "Make of everything you do a sacrifice." And Our Lady told us to say OFTEN: "O my Jesus, it is for love of You, in reparation for the offenses against the Immaculate Heart of Mary, and for the conversion of poor sinners."

If we make of *everything we do* a "sacrifice" (which we do by the Morning Offering and when we say that little prayer taught by Our Lady), we are praying always. And, we are not only very pleasing to God (to our own benefit), but we are saving many souls.

---

[75] *Poem of the Man God,* Vol. 1, p. 163.

Chapter Twenty-Seven

THE FORMULA

*The Fatima "formula of holiness" consists
of these four things: The morning offering, the
Scapular, the Rosary, and the five first Saturdays.
By this simple formula, we give ourselves to Our
Lady and She leads us on the path of holiness...the
path to Jesus in the Sacrament of His Love.*

O ur Lady said: *"When My requests are heard,*
Russia will be converted and an era of peace will
be granted to mankind."

When I saw Sister Lucia in 1946, there was one
thing above all that I wanted to know: **What are
those requests?**

Lucia Insisted On This

Sister Lucia insisted over and over that the MAIN
request of Our Lady of Fatima, to bring about
the triumph of Her Heart, *was sanctification of our
ordinary DAILY duties.* She asked for the Rosary and
consecration to Her Immaculate Heart to help us
achieve this.

Even when asked why she did not stress the first
Saturdays, she said they were important especially as
a renewal of our purpose to sanctify all our daily
actions in a spirit of reparation. Our Lady asks us to
extend our morning offering through the day.

Recently, since the change in Russia, Sister Lucia
said that the first Saturday communions of reparation

are also increasingly urgent (as we explained in chapter twenty).

The Aids

What is very special about our Mother's visit at Fatima is that She did not simply ask us to live up to our morning offering (which of course requires avoidance of sin) but *She gave us three powerful aids: The Scapular and the Rosary and the first Saturday devotion.*

The Fatima "formula of holiness" consists of those four things: *Every day* the morning offering, the Scapular, and the Rosary; and *on first Saturdays* the Rosary with 15 minute meditation, confession, and Communion. *These are the conditions of the promised triumph.*

Just for the first three requests, Our Lady promised the conversion of Russia. Now, for all four, She

On the steps of the Blue Army International Center at Fatima, the delegates pose with bishops and priests after an international meeting.

promises *an end to the wave of evil engulfing the world!* She promises an "era of peace for mankind!"

When Cardinal Vidal asked Sister Lucia (interview of Oct. 11, 1993) if the apostolate (of these four conditions) fulfilled Our Lady's wishes, she said that it did. Then she added:

"The Virgin is interested in everything (the entire pledge), but particularly in the Communion of reparation."

"Everything" is so little! All four requests are so easy! *Yet only to the degree that we know about them will we properly value them.*

We invite the reader to ask for our booklet on *the importance of the first Saturdays* which bears the title of Lucia's own words of Oct. 11, 1993: *"Fatima Has Just Begun."* It is available from LAF or the 101 Foundation.

But now a word about something extraordinary Sister Lucia said about the Scapular and the Rosary:

The Scapular and Rosary

After explaining why Our Lady appeared in Her final vision at Fatima *as Our Lady of the Scapular* ("Because She wants everyone to wear it; it is the sign of consecration to Her Immaculate Heart"), she added: *"The Scapular and the Rosary are inseparable."*[76]

When things are inseparable, usually something bonds and links them together.

In the case of the Scapular and the Rosary, that bond *is the Immaculate Heart of Mary.* One speaks to Her; the other makes us aware that She is listening.

If the Rosary is to be effective, we must be aware that Our Lady *is listening* to all those prayers. The

---

[76] This statement was in a book published by Lucia's own convent. It was the Portuguese translation of my own book *Sign of Her Heart* made by the sister who handled Lucia's English correspondence. The original statement was made by Lucia in an interview with the V. Rev. Howard Rafferty, O.Carm., which he recorded.

Scapular devotion makes us aware of Our Lady's nearness to us...that *She is listening to our every word.*

Too often, the Rosary we say becomes a repetition of words rather than a real prayer, a real conversation with Our Lady.

So, to the words of the Rosary, *we add a wordless devotion*...the Scapular profession of consecration to Our Lady without words...a "heart to heart" devotion. And this complements and completes the devotion of the Rosary.

This "heart to heart" devotion is "inseparable" from the saying of the Rosary properly, because it is the sign that our hearts are consecrated to our Mother's Immaculate Heart. And it is this combination which we call the special "gift" of Fatima.

Our Lady is a practical mother. She not only asks us to pray but She supplies special help. And that special help is not only beads to count prayers but also a special consecration to Her Immaculate Heart, helping us be aware that She is close, She is listening.

All the Tenderness of Her Heart

To realize this, it is important to realize that the Scapular is a very special act of consecration. It is quasi-liturgical. Most acts of consecration we may make by ourselves, but this one is made through a priest, who has a special faculty for this.[77] It is a consecration similar to that made by one who enters a religious order and receives a special religious habit. That is why after the first Scapular is blessed and imposed by the priest, subsequent Scapulars do not have to be blessed because it is the *person* who has been consecrated, and it is forever.

St. Claude de la Colombiere, who was chosen by Jesus to make known the revelations of His Sacred

---

[77] Formerly, this faculty could be obtained only from the Carmelites, but it is now included in the diocesan faculties of all priests.

Heart, said that in giving us the Scapular, "Our Lady reveals all the tenderness of Her Heart."

She promises us what She promised the children of Fatima: that She will take us to Heaven. She promises to bring us to the Sacred Heart of Her Son in this life, so that we may be with Him forever in Heaven. And by that promise, attached to the Scapular, She gives us a sign of constant faith, hope, and love...

Even when I sleep, the Scapular professes that I believe in God, I believe in Heaven and Hell, I believe in Jesus, and that Mary is His Mother and mine... Oh, so many truths are professed by the simple wearing of this sign of Our Lady's promise!

And what a wonderful profession of hope! The Scapular says at every moment that I hope, by Our Lady's intercession, I shall get to Heaven!

Finally, the Scapular, the "wordless devotion," says that I want to go to Heaven. I want to be with God forever. And that shows that I love Him.

Oh, what precious gifts of our loving Mother are the Rosary and the Scapular! And yet how few appreciate them!

We conclude by repeating again what Pope John Paul II said in a special letter issued on Oct. 1, 1997,[78] for the 80th anniversary of the miracle of Fatima:

"Beneath Her maternal mantle, *which extends from Fatima over the whole world,* humanity senses anew its longing for the Father's House and for His Bread" (cf. Lk. 15:17).

In the same letter, the Pope said God has given us a refuge in these days...a refuge from the tidal wave of evil. He said that refuge is Her Immaculate Heart. And Lucia said we enter that refuge by living our morning offering, with the aid of the Scapular and the Rosary.

Again, in the same letter of October 1997, which we do not tire of repeating, His Holiness said:

---

[78] *Osservatore Romano, Oct. 29, 1997*

"On the threshold of the third millennium, as we observe the signs of the times of this 20th century, Fatima is certainly one of the greatest."

He added that it is not a great sign just because of the miracle. He said it is one of the greatest signs of these times "because *its message announces many of the later events and conditions them on the response to its appeals.*"

The greatest gift given to us at Fatima is "a way out." After we are shown that we face the alternative of annihilation of nations or an era of peace for mankind, we are given *specific conditions* to avoid the first and to hasten the second.

The Extra Request

As we have said, the specific conditions to turn back the tide of evil and bring about the triumph of Our Lady are: Consecration to the Immaculate Heart of Mary (the Scapular); prayer (the Rosary); and sanctification of daily duties (the morning offering).

In addition to these basic requirements, Our Lady said, in 1917, that She would "come back" to make another request.

Ten years passed. By then (1927), Fatima had been approved. She came back as promised to ask that *on the first Saturday* of five consecutive months we would make a *Communion of reparation,* having gone to *confession,* and having on the same day said *the Rosary* and meditated on its mysteries for *fifteen minutes.*

It would seem that the most salutary way of making this last response, and the one most pleasing to the Hearts of Jesus and Mary, is the First Friday– First Saturday vigil of which we spoke above.

Four Great Promises

Our Lady promises the triumph of Her Immaculate Heart with *"an era of peace for mankind"* if enough of us respond. And this great promise in itself should be sufficient incentive to do all Our Lady asks.

Not only did Our Lady shed tears in Akita where She revealed the rest of the secret of Fatima, but more than thirty times, the International Pilgrim Virgin, shown here, has wept. The tears of Our Mother call out to us!

But in addition to promising an "era of peace to mankind," Our Lady has given us three *personal* promises:

Those who fulfill **the basic Fatima pledge** may have:

1) Assurance of *salvation;*

2) *Liberation from Purgatory soon after death* (usually understood to mean the first Saturday);[79]

3) To those who make **the five first Saturdays,** She promises: "I will assist at the hour of your death *with all the graces and aid necessary.*"

These promises confirm that this formula consisting of sanctification of daily duty (Morning Offering), prayer (Rosary), and consecration (Scapular) is a "sure fire" formula of holiness. Simple though it is, those who follow it will become saints.

St. Alphonsus Liguori, a Doctor of the Church, went so far as to say that we may *"hope not to go to Purgatory at all"* if in addition to the conditions of the Sabbatine Privilege (which we can fulfill just by following this formula) we *"do a little more."*

Does not adding the five first Saturday devotion, to the basic formula, offer us this great hope? When they exhumed the body of St. Alphonsus forty years after

---

[79] This is the Sabbatine Privilege which was promulgated by Pope John XXII in 1324 and subsequently ratified by several Popes, most recent being Pope Pius XI who called this "the greatest of all our privileges from the Mother of God, extending even after death." The conditions for the privilege are the wearing of the Scapular, chastity according to one's state in life, and the Little Office of the Blessed Virgin. The latter may be commuted by any priest to the Rosary. Most of the Fatima Apostolate pledge forms have a box which can be checked to obtain this commutation. Please note that St. Alphonsus, Doctor of the Church, said that those who do "a little more" than the basic requirements for the privilege, *may hope "not to go to Purgatory at all."* Perhaps this may be the hope of those who not only keep the basic pledge but also make the five first Saturdays.

his death, in the midst of the corruption of all else corruptible, they found his brown Scapular perfectly preserved. It seemed to cry out from the tomb the affirmation of that great statement of this Doctor of the Church concerning the Sabbatine Privilege:

"If we do a little more than Our Lady asks, can we not hope that we will not go to Purgatory at all?"

The formula *works*. It is tried and true. By this simple formula we give ourselves to Our Lady and She leads us to the Sacraments, She unites us to Her Son.

The Two Hearts

Briefly, from time to time, we have mentioned the First Friday-First Saturday vigils as ideal for honoring together the Sacred Heart of Jesus and the Immaculate Heart of Mary. We have also spoken of the beautiful term introduced by Pope John Paul II: *The Alliance of the Two Hearts.*

As we come to the end of this little book, I would not want the reader to think that we consider the Fatima Pledge (which is now promoted, not only by the Blue Army, but also by other apostolates) to be the peak, when it is the *beginning* of holiness. This is highlighted when the pledge and the first Friday/first Saturday communions of reparation are brought into special focus *upon the family.*

The Rosary has been shown over and over to heal families and to keep them together. And the Scapular unites the family in Our Lady's Immaculate Heart.

In a letter to a cousin, who was married at Lourdes, St. Therese wrote to the newlyweds that *the marriage vow made them two in one* flesh and *the Scapular made them two in one heart.*

The two hearts of husband and wife, when in covenant with the Immaculate Heart of Mary, are more deeply in covenant with each other in Our Lady's protective love. *The Scapular is the principal devotion of covenant with Mary.* The whole family is placed, by the Scapular, beneath Our Lady's mantle, in Her protective love.

Sister Lucia said Our Lady appeared with the Scapular in the final vision of Fatima "because She wants everyone to wear it." Then, Sister Lucia added: *"As Pope Pius XII said, the Scapular is our sign of consecration to Her Immaculate Heart."*

Pope Paul VI said, in application of Par. 67 of *Lumen Gentium*, that the two devotions MOST to be fostered now are the Rosary and the Scapular. This is the direction given by the Council, applied by the Pope of the Council. These are the two practical means offered by Our Lady of Fatima to place souls on the path to holiness...the path to the triumph of Her Immaculate Heart.

We reach perfection through our daily sacrifices for love of God. Our Lady came at Fatima to help us, offering the refuge of Her Immaculate Heart as She held out to us Her Rosary and Her Scapular.

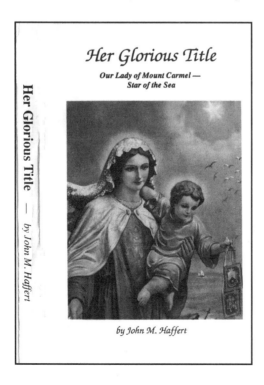

Her Glorious Title

Our Lady of Mount Carmel —
Star of the Sea

Her Glorious Title — by John M. Haffert

by John M. Haffert

Chapter Twenty-Eight

POST SCRIPT

We have built the atom bombs. God has entrusted "the Mother" with His message to save us from using them. In his Oct. 13, 1997 Fatima letter, Pope John Paul II explained that Our Lady came "to save man from himself."

Following is a letter sent to my sister, Sister Therese of the Queen of Carmel, D.C., on January 1, 1998.

Dearest Sister,

This is New Year's day. We had a partial vigil which began at 9:00 last night and ushered in the New Year with midnight Mass on this feast of Our Lady's Divine Maternity.

I did not get to bed until 3:00 this morning. Four hours later, my first thought on waking was to write to you to say: *May this New Year, the Year of the Sanctifier, be a year of transforming Grace with blessings beyond your fondest anticipation.*

You were in my prayers. Especially at the moment of benediction. As I do at every benediction of the Blessed Sacrament, I asked Our Lord to bless my dearest sister.

Do you remember the long "letter" I wrote to you in July of 1996? Your accident may dim the remembrance, but it happened that on July 7, I thought I was on my deathbed, and suddenly Bishop Hastrich and Bishop Venancio were there telling me that I still had work to do and that I was to write down what was happening to me at that time. I protested that it would be a waste. And they reminded me that I was intending at that moment to write a long letter to you for your Feast Day...

I wrote you that long letter. It was still in my computer but was almost completely forgotten until a couple of weeks ago, when I decided to look at it again.

Although much of it seemed trivial, there were facts about the new dogma, about the recognition of the Queenship of Mary, and about the Fatima apostolate, which seemed really important. So I decided to edit the letter into a little book.

Thus, the last book of my life will be essentially a letter to my dear sister, who entered Carmel at the very beginning of my apostolate and who has been its main victory-winner in these many years of spiritual warfare.

One in Their Sacred Hearts,
Your loving brother...

Post Script to the Reader:

You might be tempted to think that in writing this letter to my sister in the Boston Carmel, on New Year's day of 1998, I might have had in mind to use it here. I did not. But since all this book was originally based on a letter to her, this letter (telling her of my decision to write it) seems the best way to end it.

What I was about on 7/7/96 was what I had been about for fifty years: **To try to shake the world by the shoulders and say: "Listen to the warning and message God has sent** *the Mother* **to tell you!"**

My sister knew that. She was my spiritual partner. Since she prayed and suffered to make it all happen, I felt obliged to tell her (especially once a year on her Feast Day) what I was doing at the moment.

But was there any value in my having taken the 7/7/96 "Heavenly voices" seriously enough to expand the letter, begun that day, into this book?

One thing I came to realize is that I get so absorbed in what I am doing *now,* that a few months later, I tend to forget what was happening *then.* Only eight months before 7/7/96, I had almost succeeded in having the film *State of Emergency* released. But I had already forgotten. The flights of the Queen of the World plane from cities all over America, which made it possible for so many thousands to witness Fatima for themselves, now seemed something of the dim past.

So, it is quite certain that if I had not thought I was being told by Heavenly visitors to write about what I was doing as of 7/7/96, it would all soon have been forgotten.

Hope for the Blue Army

Although it seemed especially important to write about my concerns for the *immediate* future of the U.S. Blue Army, I would not want the reader to think that, because of those concerns, the U.S. Blue Army was on the way to ruin. Quite the opposite.

The Holy Father had intervened. The Blue Army now had canonical standing with a constitution drafted under the direction of the Bishop (a Rome trained expert in Canon Law)[80] who had been sent by the Vatican. We can hope the Blue Army will be of

---

[80] The Most Rev. Edward Egan, D.D., then bishop of Bridgeport, CT.

The Queen of the World plane flew directly from cities across America to Lisbon up to four times a week carrying up to 22,000 Blue Army pilgrims to Fatima in a single year.

greater service to the Church in the future than in the past if the national membership *lives up to the obligations of its new constitution* by electing trustees who will see that it fulfills its true purpose.[81]

At the same time I repeat now, as in the chapter on the Lay Apostolate, the joy and hope we all must feel in the spontaneous explosion of lay apostolates in the U.S., like Maxkol, the Centers of Peace, 101 Foundation, Communion Mary, Alliance of the Two Hearts, Pilgrim Virgins, Queen of the Americas, and of the *dozens* of individual apostles like Bud

---

[81] Blue Army members have a right to financial statements and to *copies of the minutes of the meetings of the executive committee.* Diocesan delegates should require these documents, without which they cannot vote responsibly.

McFarland, Joey Lomangino, Dave Blum, Ted and Maureen Flynn, Tom Petrisko, Mary Ann Ferrugia, Tom Fahy, Tony Weibel, Marietta Canning, Bob and Celeste Behling, Mark Miravalle, Dan Lynch...and so many more that it seems unfair to name a few because *this book could be filled with their names.* And, the same explosion of apostolic zeal is to be seen in other countries, like Anatol Kaszczuk in Poland, Kevin Morley in Australia, and on and on.

Blue Army a Starting Point

Most of these zealous persons were Blue Army members. Some (like Dr. Turton, Anatol Kaszczuk, etc.) had been or still were Blue Army leaders. Many testify that *their active involvement in the life of the Church **began with the Blue Army.***

And that is as Our Lady intends. The Blue Army pledge, so simple and easy, draws us to Our Lady and *She transforms us,* as She did the children of Fatima. Bishop Venancio, second bishop of Fatima, said:

"The task of the Blue Army of Our Lady of Fatima consists in making known to the whole world the message of Fatima, by all the means at its disposal, so that men of all nations will realize it in their personal lives... It does not address itself to an elite class. Its practices are contained in those *duties of the Christian which are rooted in the Gospel.*"[82]

The Blue Army gives us Our Lady's warning and message and asks only the BASIC response: Extending the morning offering through the day with the help of the Scapular and Rosary as first steps on a journey of holiness. The first Saturday devotion follows, and soon we have saints. And they will renew the Church.

In *The Dogma and the Triumph* (Queenship Publishing Co., 1988, 153 pgs.), Dr. Mark Miravalle writes, as we mentioned once before:

---

[82] *Dear Bishop,* p. 322.

"In an authentically Marian sense, we have reached the fullness of time. We have reached that which has been called the climax of the age of Mary, an apex, a summit, a high point which has been preceded by many holy events and great saints and teachers." To this he added:

"We, who are consecrated as 'Totus Tuus' servants and slaves of our Mother Coredemptrix, must now begin anew our prayer and labor for the Triumph of the Immaculate Heart of Mary! Even with the eventual definition of the last Marian Dogma, members of *Vox Populi,* and all hearts consecrated to the Immaculate Heart of Mary, must continue to participate as a Marian family, a Marian remnant, in bringing forth all components of the great Triumph of our Mother which leads to the Eucharistic Reign of the Most Sacred Heart of Jesus.

"We have a great responsibility, one which will not be easy to fulfill considering the state of the world and the many storms which rock the Church" (pg. 73).

"God has Entrusted to Her the Peace of the World"
— Jacinta

In an earlier chapter, I said that the book NOW, which was just coming off the press on 7/7/96, was like a last sputtering of a lifelong effort to shake the world by the shoulders with the warning cry of Fatima and Akita.

Until our last breath, we cannot refrain from trying to tell all the world the good news: We deserve God's chastisement, but He has entrusted the peace of the world to our Mother, who is Queen of the World and crushes Satan.